M000035969

Kristin,

Everything you need to create your
Aligned Abundance & manifest your
dreams is already inside you!

Stacey

Our deepest fear is not that we are inadequate. Our deepest fear is that we are powerful beyond measure. It is our light, not our darkness that most frightens us. We ask ourselves, Who am I to be brilliant, gorgeous, talented, fabulous? Actually, who are you not to be? You are a child of God. Your playing small does not serve the world. There is nothing enlightened about shrinking so that other people won't feel insecure around you. We are all meant to shine, as children do. We were born to make manifest the glory of God that is within us. It is not just in some of us; it is in everyone and as we let our own light shine, we unconsciously give other people permission to do the same. As we are liberated from our own fear, our presence automatically liberates others.

~ Marianne Williamson, A Return to Love: Reflections on the Principles of "A Course in Miracles"

Be A Boss & Fire That Bitch

Quiet Your Inner Critic & Finally
Believe You're GOOD ENOUGH!

STACY RASKE

BE A BOSS & FIRE THAT BITCH
QUIET YOUR INNER CRITIC & FINALLY BELIEVE YOU'RE GOOD ENOUGH!

Published by
Empowered Overthinker Publishing
601 Venture Drive, #200
Morgantown, WV 26508

COPYRIGHT © 2019 BY STACY RASKE

All rights reserved. No part of this book may be used, reproduced, stored in a retrieval system, or transmitted by any means—electronic, mechanical, photocopy, microfilm, recording, or otherwise—without written permission from the publisher, except in the case of brief quotations embodied in critical articles or reviews. For more information, address: stacy@stacyraske.com.

Printed in the United States of America

ISBN: 978-0-578-56387-9

Cover design by Randolph Scott
Cover photo by Anthony Sparks
Author photos by Lauren Webster

www.StacyRaske.com

DISCLAIMER AND/OR LEGAL NOTICES

While the publisher and author have used their best efforts in preparing this book, they make no representations or warranties with respect to the accuracy or completeness of the contents of this book. The advice and strategies contained herein may not be suitable for your situation. You should consult a professional where appropriate. Neither the publisher nor the author shall be liable for any loss of profit or any other commercial damages, including but not limited to special, incidental, consequential, or other damages. The purchaser or reader of this publication assumes responsibility for the use of these materials and information. Adherence to all applicable laws and regulations, both advertising and all other aspects of doing business in the United States or any other jurisdiction, is the sole responsibility of the purchaser or reader.

This book is intended to provide accurate information with regards to the subject matter covered. However, the Author and the Publisher accept no responsibility for inaccuracies or omissions, and the Author and Publisher specifically disclaim any liability, loss, or risk, whether personal, financial, or otherwise, that is incurred as a consequence, directly or indirectly, from the use and/or application of any of the contents of this book.

ADVANCE PRAISE

"When I started working with her, [. . .] I set some pretty lofty goals. In the back of my mind, I thought, "Yeah right, no way am I doing this". However, over the next three months, I put in the work and not only achieved my business goals, closed on my dream home, and allowed myself to break through some pretty big barriers I had built, but I changed the way I viewed myself, and I was able to learn how to control the way I perceived situations. All of this allows me to be better in control of my thoughts and my inner critic. [. . .] I have been able to shift to more empowering thoughts, which has changed my life. I cannot say enough about what she has done for me and the person she has helped me become."

— Jennifer Wilson, Mortgage Lender & Women's Advocate

"[W]ith Stacy's help, I have finally gotten in the headspace to lose weight and find my healthy side—being down 50 lbs. and 40 inches in just about 6 months! Additionally, I have the tools and resources to thrive in my personal life and work-life! Finding a balance between loving myself, family, and work has been made easier when I define and stick to my boundaries, own my schedule, and honor my inner badass! I have an amazing emotional toolkit that I have from my time working with Stacy and reach into it often to stay on track. Let's be honest, life is a journey, and we often need to review past lessons. I find myself going back to the lessons from Stacy and continuing to implement those methods to better self-love and empowerment. I count meeting Stacy as one of my life's biggest blessings. Thank you, Stacy, for helping me find myself and bloom!"

— Lindsay Williams, Real Estate Broker and Post-Cancer Blogger

"I came to Stacy with the goal of starting my own business so that I could be home with my family more. With this goal, I brought a complete lack of entrepreneurial knowledge and even more so, a lack of confidence to actually achieve my goal. [. . .] Stacy didn't "tell" me how to work through my lack of confidence. Instead, she gave me the tools to discover why I lacked confidence, and then she allowed my journey to unfold. [. . .} Out of everything I have accomplished with Stacy, I am most grateful that I have learned to make my own life decisions, despite what people may think of my decisions. For the first time in my life, I am living for me, and by living for me, I am a better person, mom, and wife. Most of all, because I believe in myself, I now believe that my possibilities in life are endless. Because of my work with Stacy, I am now launching my very own business as a MOMS Mentor™ and spreading light to moms who have lost a sense of who they are after having children!"

— Meghann Kolb, Holistic Coach, Yoga Instructor & MOMS Mentor

TABLE OF CONTENTS

FOREWORD

Over the years, I've met a lot of people who claim to have the skills necessary to help you overcome your inner mindset struggles. The ones most worth listening to have built their "expertise" in the trenches while struggling and overcoming countless trials. Their valuable knowledge comes directly from experiencing and overcoming some serious life situations. As you'll see in the raw personal stories that Stacy shares in this powerful book, her advice is based on her real-life experiences that she overcame and learned from.

I met Stacy Raske through my mastermind program, Traffic & Leads Masters. I haven't known Stacy for more than a year or two BUT from the moment I met her, I knew she was special. Maybe that's because we're cut from the same cloth—type A personalities refusing to give up on our dreams—or maybe it's because she's one of those people who everyone is naturally drawn to. Either way, she's inspiring! I was excited to help Stacy with her digital marketing because it meant that more people would have the opportunity to learn from her. Consider yourself lucky that she wrote this powerful book so you can experience her extraordinary energy!

In my experience working with entrepreneurs over the past 12 years, I have seen many business owners who have the skills and talent to seriously reach their goals, but they are held back by one simple thing: themselves. To succeed in business, you need to have a dream and be able to fail before you achieve success. The problem is, when your mind is full of fear, stress, and self-doubt, you will never stay focused enough to achieve your dreams.

I'll be straight-up: this book doesn't pull any punches. And if you're the kind of person who has a loud inner critic or is suffering from uncertainty, avoidance, exhaustion, slow growth, procrastination, perfectionism, or anything in between, then you NEED to read this book.

All of those things are usually pretty tough to talk about. More often than not, we internalize them and don't let anyone else know what we're going through. I have personally been there more times than I can count throughout my twelve-year career in digital marketing. It's hard. It's really, really hard, but Stacy approaches these topics with a kind of honesty that surprises and disarms you.

Each section of this book begins with a personal anecdote about Stacy, so you know she's not full of fluff. She's been where you are. She understands what you're going through. She doesn't sugarcoat any of her experiences; when reading these stories, you realize that she's the real deal and you can trust what she's saying. She proves herself to you, time and time again.

The most valuable part of this book is definitely her advice. The tactics she gives you aren't like anything you've ever heard before. Don't expect the usual "take a break," or "drink more water," or, "meditate," or "exercise." While those are all important aspects of self-care, Stacy gets into the meat of your problems and asks the tough, hard-to-talk-about questions so you can learn why you're getting in your own way.

She'll teach you how to take back your life. Throughout this book, she'll give you actionable items that you can do right now, today, whether it's a specific question you need to break down and address or a new method to utilize (like her Empowered Overthinker Method™, which I can't WAIT for you to learn about!)

You'll also get a chance to break down what she's given you and collect your thoughts on how it applies to your own situation thanks to the journal prompts that conclude each chapter. Trust me... the journaling is a HUGE help; my own journal is pretty damn full after finishing this book!

The bottom line is if you've picked up this book, chances are, it's for a reason. If you picked up this book, it means you're ready. You're ready to finally make lasting change, to get out of that brain fog and be present for every aspect of your life. Stacy can help you get to that new, rejuvenated, motivated, hungry-for-life place that you want to be in so badly. The fact that you've decided to start is a huge step in the right direction.

And Stacy would agree with me when I say we're so proud of you for taking that leap.

Lindsey Anderson – "One-Click Lindsey"
www.trafficandleads.com

INTRODUCTION

And you're stuck...AGAIN!

But let's talk about WHY you're stuck. The REAL reason you're struggling to succeed.

No need to BS yourself. Your time is valuable (even though you likely haven't been respecting it, but I'll get into that later). No time for fluff or people-pleasing here.

WHY YOU NEED THIS BOOK

You see the signs in your business—procrastination, perfection, avoidance, slow growth, feast or famine, struggling to find quality leads, working really hard with little or no return, not being consistent or following through, and not reaching your goals or the income you'd like.

You see the signs in your life—exhausted, unfocused, low energy, poor quality sleep, imbalance in your relationships, calendar out of control, pulled in too many directions, feeling reactive, lots of guilt and self-judgment fueling your terrible inner critic.

You're tired of never feeling like you're GOOD ENOUGH. Constantly getting in your own way, feeling trapped in your sabotage cycles and stuck beneath an invisible burden stopping you from being your best. You feel like an impostor compared to what others see in you, and your never-ending list of *shoulds* keeps you feeling guilty for not being better. Your self-doubt leads to overthinking and scarcity in every part of your life and business.

No Time, No Money, No Clients, No Connection, No Confidence.

There are a ton of gurus and influencers teaching you how to plan and prepare to get your goals. They show you how to bullet journal, mind map, visualize and vision board your way into manifesting your goals and dreams. The problem is that they are NOT teaching you how to follow through and make those dreams a reality. Those concepts are great, I use many myself and include a few in this book. However, they leave you in what I call Preparation Purgatory! Circling around the far outside of your goals, always planning and getting ready without ever taking action to make it happen. Keep in mind, it's not necessarily direct action on your goal.

As you'll discover in this book, action is more often focused on how you're feeling and who you're being rather than efforting or forcing your success. And most importantly, these concepts don't address how to heal the root issues and beliefs keeping you stuck in sabotage and purgatory in the first place.

This book is a comprehensive how-to guide to finally believing you're good enough and allowing yourself to be successful.

MY STORY

Until recently, I spent my entire life searching for approval from others and validation through achievement. Eventually, I discovered this was driven by my search for the love and connection I desperately wanted from my parents when I was a child. Both of my parents were emotionally unavailable to varying degrees, challenged with the very limited or dysfunctional coping toolkit they learned dealing with their respective childhood traumas.

My mom did the best she could with what she had, although her walls prevented the deepest connection and closeness we both craved. My father, who falls on the narcissistic spectrum, was completely walled off and unavailable for connection, and he was inconsistent in my life since they divorced when I was two. Each had their emotional baggage that blocked them from opening up, even though they are both really good people with huge hearts. Moving around a lot as a child, even between parents, amplified my struggle, so I never felt the safety or stability *I* longed for, as well. This feeling peaked when my mom moved away, basically leaving me homeless at 16 years old with no choice but to crash with friends so I could finish high school. This laid the foundation for my feelings of rejection and abandonment as a child that spilled over into adulthood.

It's funny to now know the driving force for all my achievement was simply searching for the "I'm proud of you" and "I love you" from my parents, especially my dad. I know they told me, but it's hard for kids to believe it if they don't feel it. We do that all the time: say one thing, but our energy and emotion say something COMPLETELY different. My need to be perfect and always get external validation in some way started early in life. I was always crafting myself into the person I thought I *should* be to avoid rejection or abandonment.

This has permeated EVERY aspect of my life...

Relationships, my time in the military, my corporate career, and my health, and it fueled my ever-increasingly terrible inner critic.

My need to CONTROL everything in my life, curating who I was so others would approve, and taking care of everyone else, eventually led to my rock bottom moment where I completely fell apart. I felt alone in my struggle, focusing more and more inward, self-medicating my thoughts and feelings due to a lack of coping skills. I was constantly giving my power away to external things and people because I had NO boundaries. At the root, I never felt good enough because I didn't know how to love myself. I believed it had to come from outside.

My rock bottom moment happened at the end of 2014. It was the first time in a LONG time that I became aware of what I was thinking and how that was driving my behavior. This moment occurred to me as I stood in front of my kitchen pantry pulling food out and shoving it into my mouth. There I was, bawling my eyes out and chasing the food with a bottle of wine when suddenly it dawned on me what I was doing.

What I was feeling finally came into my awareness. The voice in my head said, "I'm trying to make my outside look as ugly as I feel inside."

There was nothing about who I was being that felt real or authentic. I was miserable. I didn't know this person I'd become, pretending to be someone to please others. Everything I'd been doing over the last 10 years or so is because it's who and what I thought I *should* be. I was overwhelmed with depression and anxiety, I'd lost my career, my marriage was falling apart, PTSD cycles kept me near-total shutdown. Because I had NO healthy coping skills for my thoughts and feelings, I spent a lifetime avoiding them. The family pattern I learned was to numb out and avoid my feelings with food, alcohol, television, social media, games, meds, and drugs. In fact, in my worst moments, I was even engaging in self-harm. Anything to change how I was feeling in the moment because I had NO coping skills to deal with any of it. I. HATED. MYSELF.

The voice in my head, my inner critic, was RUTHLESS and constantly found evidence to support my self-hatred. I numbed out because I felt so OUT OF CONTROL inside. As I mentioned, my coping skills were very limited, so I didn't know how to handle the burden I was carrying. I simply reacted to everything because I was completely out of control. So, my journey from that moment on focused on building the necessary foundation and toolkit to take control of ME.

The reason I share when my rock bottom moment occurred is to highlight how massive transformation doesn't take as long as we believe or expect it will. When looking at your big vision, it can seem overwhelming and feel like it'll take *forever* to manifest your dreams. As I write this book in 2019, I've come a LONG way in only five short years, transforming EVERY aspect of my life, health, relationships and career. And to be honest, it would have happened even faster had I invested in help and a book like this earlier in my journey.

WHY I WROTE THIS BOOK

I wrote this book so you know you're not alone in your struggle. So many high-achieving women have such profoundly similar stories. The details may be different, but the symptoms are the same…tons of self-doubt and a mean inner critic. Throughout this book, I share very real, raw stories as examples of how this old programming affected me personally, and later as an entrepreneur. I've also included a few powerful client stories as well.

This book is designed to help you understand WHY you're getting in your own way, uncovering and healing the root problems driving your control issues, fear, worry, and nasty inner critic. It will also help you identify all the subtle ways you're sabotaging yourself, too. More importantly, this book shows you HOW to effectively address the root issue rather than just focusing on the symptoms, so you can get into action and reach your goals. You'll be able to build a solid foundation and move forward with confidence so you can experience consistent results in your life and business.

I share a simple and powerful process for quieting your inner critic and finally believing you're GOOD ENOUGH. It's what my clients and I use every day because it works! This is a step-by-step guide to building a powerful connection to you and transforming your relationship with your inner critic. I'll help you understand the root of your struggles and decipher the message in your sabotage. Ultimately, my goal is to help you understand that this voice doesn't have to run your life and business anymore, allowing you to make the powerful shift from high-achiever to high-performer. You can take your power back, feel in control of YOU, and finally believe you're GOOD ENOUGH to be successful!

You may be surprised, but you're very successful at manifesting! In fact, you're getting everything you EXPECT. The problem is that your expectations are not aligned with what you want. You expect yourself to fail, sabotage, and not be good enough, and you get EXACTLY what you expect.

This book will help you understand those expectations and how they're keeping you stuck, and more importantly, shift your relationship with YOU to create expectations that are aligned with what you want to do and what you want to have in your life and business. But most importantly, it will help you become the person you want to BE.

WHAT TO EXPECT

As a fellow overthinker, I want to know the HOW and the WHY of everything. I want to understand WHY I'm stuck or sabotaging myself and, of course, what to do about it. I want to know HOW to take control of me and make lasting changes. Plus, if you've ever gotten stuck simply because you didn't know HOW to make your dream, idea, or vision come to life, I've got you! In the past, I've shut down just because I had no idea HOW to make my dream a reality rather than simply trusting the universe to help me make it happen. Getting stuck when you don't know HOW is just another control issue fueled by our self-doubt and need to avoid failure.

I've structured the book so, after reading, you can easily reference sections later.

Here's the layout for each chapter:

- **STORY**: I'll start each chapter with a personal story that sets the stage in a relatable way to what will be discussed in the chapter. Then I'll share a business-focused story from myself or one of my client's.

- **SYMPTOMS**: This is where I discuss the struggles and challenges you're experiencing in your life and business.

- **SOURCE**: In this section, I discuss the root issues fueling those symptoms and the source of those issues. This is the explanation of WHY you're having those symptoms and struggles.

- **SOLUTION**: This section is where I explain HOW to fix it and what to address. Not knowing how to do something is one of the biggest reasons we don't move forward.

- **EMPOWERED ACTION**: You must be willing to DO something different to get a different result. I share specific exercises, journal prompts, and resources I've created to take targeted action in addressing the root issues fueling your critic and get you moving forward with confidence. Plus, I encourage you to connect in the Facebook group with specific wins, lessons, challenges, or questions.

JOURNAL

Also, I encourage you to have a dedicated journal or notebook to use as you're going through this book. You will gain so many powerful insights and new understandings of yourself simply by reading, so it's great to quickly jot down those gold nuggets of wisdom. Plus, there are journal prompts in each chapter and writing exercises throughout the book. If you don't already journal regularly, I encourage you to do daily journaling while you're going through the journey this book will take you on, both within the pages and using the outside resources I recommend.

BEYOND THIS BOOK

Throughout the book, I have suggested resources and tools. I've gathered these powerful resources in one location to support your use of this book. Basically, I want to make this process as simple as possible to ensure your success. As I mentioned, each chapter will have Empowered Action steps to take, and I've provided a tool, resource or exercise to support almost every chapter.

CHAPTER RESOURCES

Go to https://www.stacyraske.com/bookresources for free access to the resources suggested in the Empowered Action section of each chapter.

GROUP SUPPORT

As high-achievers with a terrible inner critic, we usually struggle alone since we already feel like we must do everything ourselves (Hey, if you want it done right...LOL). We bear the burden, believing that we *can't* ask for help or that no one will understand what we're going through. As you'll discover throughout the book, I understand this first-hand, so I've created communities of like-minded people to connect and support each other.

My free Facebook group, **the Aligned Abundance Lab** (https://www.facebook.com/groups/alignedabundancelab), is for purpose-driven female entrepreneurs who are working to quiet their inner critic, reduce sabotage, and be their best to create the life and business of their dreams. Join the community to connect, ask questions, share wins, and get support or accountability when you're struggling. I share specific trainings only in this group.

If you're not a fit for that group, I've got you covered. Join my other free community, **the Empowered Overthinker's Society** (https://www.facebook.com/groups/empoweredoverthinkers), with all the same benefits as the other group.

As you go through the book and use the tools, you're going to learn a lot about yourself and have some amazing insights. Feel free to share those wins and lessons, as well as ask questions, in the Facebook group.

CHAPTER 1: WHO'S THAT BITCH?

PERSONAL

There's never enough because I'm not enough.

The first scarcity in my life was love from my parents, especially my dad since I didn't see him regularly. As I mentioned previously, they were unable to deeply connect with me due to their walls and emotional baggage. I was a very empathetic, intuitive child from the start, very aware and highly sensitive to those around me, but no one ever talked about thoughts and feelings. For the most part, we only had surface-level communication.

The challenges with a real connection in those key relationships planted the seed early in life that I was not enough, that there was something wrong with me. I wasn't enough for my dad to be around consistently. There wasn't enough love, so I had to work hard to get attention. Ultimately, I ended up with a deep core belief that I wasn't worthy, lovable or enough as myself because of feeling rejected and abandoned. I always sought attention and approval from those around me by being as others expected me to be or doing big things.

I remember learning early on that I got attention and approval when I was who others expected me to be. More importantly, behaving as expected was how I avoided verbal and emotional abuse from my father. By acting a certain way, getting good grades, or achieving in athletics or arts, I got the attention I wanted from one or both of my parents. Also, by being who I thought others wanted, it was easy to make friends since I moved around so much. I created a version of myself—who I thought I *should* be for people to like me—with lies and stories. I crafted a person who wasn't myself because I didn't have any confidence in the real me. The real me never seemed to be accepted by anyone. The weird thing was that I wasn't very nice to those who did know more of the real me because it triggered my fear of rejection when feeling that vulnerable. If I push them away first, then I won't get hurt by them rejecting the real me like those I craved acceptance from the most.

BUSINESS

The last pillar of my coaching certification program focused on business. They had examples of how to grow your business based on what stage of business you're in and setting your prices accordingly. What they recommended as a starting package rate blew my mind. I thought it was WAY TOO high for my area! I couldn't imagine anyone I knew would pay *that* for coaching. I believed no one would pay *me* that much. But I took the risk and did my first sales call and asked for that amount, which was strongly rejected, reinforcing my belief that no one would pay that amount. So, I started MUCH lower, at an amount less than a third of the original amount. And when I finally enrolled my first client, it was on payments! I couldn't even convince them the value of what I was offering was worth a full investment, even with a price that low.

Initially, I thought this difficulty was due to external conditions like the economics of where I lived, but it was really a reflection of my belief in myself and my value, as well as fear and scarcity around money. I didn't believe I was worth that much, so that's the energy I projected. Why would anyone want to pay me that much for my wisdom and experience when they could find a better coach, someone more trained, experienced, or just plain better.

SYMPTOMS

Of course, your inner critic is that negative voice telling you that you're not good enough to do something, or you just can't be or do or have what you desire, undermining your success from the start. But your inner critic is so much more, subtly permeating every aspect of your life and business in ways you may not even realize. Your critic keeps you trapped in cycles of sabotage like avoidance, distraction, and justifiable excuses.

It fuels control issues like perfection, procrastination, and expectation. Everything you do comes from a place of fear and lack, never having enough resources. Self-doubt and resistance prevent you from taking action toward your goals. And the longer you're stuck, the more you judge and criticize yourself for sabotaging in the first place, making you more uncomfortable and reactive.

SCARCITY

Scarcity is believing that there is a lack in everything you do or are working toward. The easiest place to see it is in your relationship with money and time, there is never enough, or you say you just don't have any. These feelings of not enough also affect other important resources, such as love, support, health, joy, and fun. It may feel like you're unloved or unsupported by your partner or family, or that you can only have a set amount of these resources because others have them in abundance. Basically, there is not enough money or success left in the world for you to have what you want. You may see this the most in your business by how you feel about charging more or showing up consistently. You're not skilled enough, trained enough, credentialed or certified enough, you need another program or strategy, or aren't good enough at what you do to do charge more. The ultimate scarcity is doubt or a lack of confidence in yourself, which affects everything from taking action to being fully present in the moment.

JUDGMENT

Comparison is an interesting method of self-judgment in which we keep ourselves feeling inferior. By focusing on what someone else has or is doing and using it to reflect what we are not doing, being, or having, we're highlighting more scarcity and how we are not enough. This is where we pick up a lot of the things we believe we *should* be doing. By comparing ourselves to other parents, couples, business owners, and measure ourselves against them, we develop a very distorted perspective. As the saying goes, we compare our worst moments against someone else's highlight reel.

Over time, it gets exhausting constantly being critical of ourselves, so we turn outward and inevitably become critical of others, especially those closest to us. We are critical of those who mirror what we criticize in ourselves, pointing out what's wrong with our partner, kids, friends, family, boss, etc. Complaining about everything and blaming others for the problems in your life, business, or relationships. We are critical of everything and everyone, constantly viewing life from a place of judgment and comparison to another time, person, or ourselves.

Even though you're so critical of yourself and others, the primary fear that drives the inner critic is worrying about what others are thinking and feeling about you. Basically, you fear judgment and rejection from them, but I'll get into that a lot more in the next chapter. Your inner critic may be the voice of someone critical of you early in life from your family of origin. Often, our first critic was one or both of our parents, especially if they were very controlling, narcissistic, or negative.

SOURCE

Stepping into an observer view of the inner critic, it's interesting to see what that voice really is and how it came to be. Every which way to Sunday, that voice tells us we are not enough. It does it in a million sneaky ways, not always focusing just on us. It can look like scarcity of resources or justifiable excuses. And of course, comparison, complaining, and criticism of others. The belief underneath that is the root of your scarcity—I AM NOT ENOUGH! Your core scarcity belief is *there is not enough because I am not enough.*

Your beliefs of not enough, unworthy, and unlovable were planted early in life. The more trauma, instability, emotional disconnect, and lack of structure you experience as a child, especially before the age of seven, the stronger those limiting beliefs become. Anything that affected your sense of safety, stability, or connection has a lasting impact on your connection to self.

Even the best parents and childhoods can still inadvertently plant the seeds of these beliefs in a child, as children internalize everything due to their worlds being very small and emotion-based. Those limiting beliefs start to drive your behavior, the construct of who you are as an individual (ego version of you), and the internal dialog with yourself (inner critic). Basically, your wounded inner child is running your life now, interfering with your goals, your relationships, your mindset and beliefs, your ability to succeed and grow your business, along with how you show up and who you are being.

CONDITIONAL

Your enoughness has been sourced externally, by achievement, validation, connection, success, love, or things. But because your feelings of worthy and good enough are from external sources, that feeling is fickle and fleeting. If the conditions aren't perfect or you don't get the return you're looking for, you don't feel good. When you don't feel enough, sabotage cycles and the inner critic flare up. These cycles can last for extended periods of time because you're looking for the next outside fix for your internal problems.

That's why the inner critic and limiting beliefs are so persistent and prevalent. We spend a lifetime looking for solutions by fueling the problem. By engaging in the habits, beliefs, and cycles that are keeping you stuck in the first place. This is also how you're constantly giving your power away to other people and external things as they control how you feel and who you are being because you're being who you think you *should* be instead of your authentic self. When outside sources have control over you instead of *you* being in control of you, you feel out of control, which fuels your need to be in control of *something*. This is why you have control issues.

REJECTION

Your ego has you constantly worrying about what others are thinking about you or if they're judging you. Ego is the constructed version of ourselves, the version of ourselves we present to avoid hurts and rejection. Especially if you grew up with a narcissistic, manipulative, or critical parent, you're being a version of you that's created as opposed to authentically expressing your truth. When the ego controls your perception of a situation, you have no chance of seeing the root cause, as the ego only sees what reaffirms its perspective and hides in self-criticism. Basically, you only see what supports your beliefs.

What you believe becomes the reality of your life experience. Your ego is the filter upon which you perceive and experience life. That's why it's so hard to break free of the filter and believe YOU ARE ENOUGH when all you see is the evidence that reinforces feeling unworthy and not enough. Even if 99% of what happens is wonderful, your filter will only focus on the 1% that supports your feeling of not good enough. You're constantly REJECTING the good from your life experience. This is why your inner critic has so much power over you and had been calling the shots in your life and business: it supports the agenda of your ego.

When it comes to the role of your inner critic as well, it's important to talk about self-rejection. In curating this version of you to be who everyone else expects you to be, instead of living your truth, you're rejecting yourself so you won't be rejected by others. This is why we're so concerned with what other people's judgments and opinions are of us. We must know who others want us to be to become that version and avoid rejection or abandonment. This rejection of our truth leads to feeling like a dichotomy, like there are two different versions of you. There is the person you show to the world, the mask you wear based on who you believe and have been taught you *should* be. Then there is the REAL you, deep down, that you don't let out. Because you reject your authentic self — the truth of who you are — it gets out in destructive ways as your inner rebel. No matter how much you reject or compartmentalize yourself, that is your truth. It's always inside of you.

AUTHENTIC SELF

Since I'm talking about connection to your authentic self, let's clarify exactly who your true, authentic self is and what connecting to it means. You are your authentic self when you're born, fully connected and aligned with God or Source because the person you're being is the expression of your soul. This is the energetic part of you, your vibrational being that helps you manifest your dreams. As a child, you express yourself freely with the skills you have; feel and connect openly; are confident, full of love, without judgment; and spend your life in the present moment. As your authentic self, you feel full, overflowing with love and enoughness as you're fully aligned. You're born with only two fears, falling and loud noises, so all your fears and limitations are learned as part of your early programming.

Over time, as a child, you also experience hurts, rejection, abandonment, and trauma, all of which wound you. Around the age of 6 or 7, your ego develops and creates your individual identity, separating you from your authentic self to protect you from the hurts you've already had and experiencing more pain. Your ego uses the coping toolkit you've learned from your family of origin to adapt who you're being to avoid more hurt. However, this begins the process of disconnect and deviation from your authentic self, which increases over time.

Connecting to and aligning with your authentic self as an adult means you must also process and heal the wounds of your inner child. As your ineffective toolkit doesn't support this, you're still avoiding the emotions and disconnected from your truth. Your alignment and expression of your soul's truth is the only way to finally believe you're good enough.

SOLUTION

CONNECTION

The path to quieting your inner critic starts with building a strong connection to you. That is the relationship that is suffering the most because you've been looking outside for answers and validation to fill the void. The more disconnected you've been from your authentic self, the more you felt unworthy and not good enough, triggering your search to fill the emptiness inside with external sources. The process of turning inward and nurturing your relationship with you can be scary and perhaps the most uncomfortable part of your journey. It was for me, as my whole life was focused on using external things, people, or achievement to feel like I was good enough. But by strengthening your connection with you and expressing more of your authentic self, you find your enoughness from within, allowing you to blossom into the amazing, successful person you're designed to be and fully live your purpose.

The only way you will ever truly feel like you're good enough and worthy of success is to learn to love yourself as a whole. That's the answer to the problem of your inner critic, like it or not—healing the wounds of your inner child and reprogramming the beliefs that you hold at your core. And you'll discover, step-by-step, throughout this book, an understanding of all the ways in which your critic is getting in the way, because awareness is the first step, along with what to do about it.

Much of this process indirectly addresses the problems you see because you'll be healing the root instead of treating the symptoms. What I mean by that is, you can't transform your relationship with time by using a new planner. The planner is addressing the symptom, how you manage your time. But your relationship with time starts with your relationship with you. If you don't have good boundaries with you and others or belief in your ability to be responsible with time, you'll have a hard time saying no to things or making you a priority.

Loving and embracing yourself as whole is perhaps the most important aspect to quieting your inner critic because you're filling your cup of enoughness. Who you're being and how you're showing up is dictated by this relationship with yourself. No longer rejecting, compartmentalizing, and editing who you are because it doesn't align with the expectations of your family, of your profession, socially, or culturally. When you're constantly judging yourself as bad or wrong, it's impossible to ever believe you're good enough for success in any part of your life or business.

EMPOWERED ACTION

RESOURCE

Download and complete the Get Outta Your Head Quick Guide.

EXERCISE

Understand your Inner Critic:

- Whose voice is your inner critic?
- Whose opinions of you do you worry about the most?
- Where did it come from?
- What triggers that voice?

JOURNAL

Where is scarcity showing up in your life?

- You don't have enough resources, like time, money, health, love, or joy.
- You're not good enough to start or finish a project (procrastination).
- You're not [insert label] enough to do that, be that, charge that. Labels: skilled, certified, experienced, trained, educated, thin, smart, pretty, etc.

CONNECT

Share your biggest discoveries and insights in the Facebook group from the resource, exercise, and journaling.

NOTES

_____

_____

_____

_____

_____

_____

_____

_____

_____

_____

_____

CHAPTER 2: SABOTAGE

PERSONAL

My default is to be in my head! Totally shocking at this point, I know. I was so in my head that it was impossible for me to be present, too focused on the past, future, or what else I needed to be doing. But I didn't want to be present. Being present meant that I had to get honest with myself about who I was being and how I really felt about myself and my life. I coasted through years of my life on autopilot. There is about a 7-year window with huge chunks missing from my memory and about 3 years I don't remember much at all. I was completely checked out! Some of this was a coping mechanism as well, to simply avoid my thoughts, feelings, and life as it was by mentally and emotionally being elsewhere. Basically, I was being my parents, checked out and emotionally unavailable.

And this was my husband's biggest frustration with me. He could feel it. I would completely disengage from my life in the evening on my phone playing games, in front of the television, with a drink in my other hand. I'd sit there all evening and not say a word to him. I wasn't present in our marriage. He got so angry with me being on my phone that sometimes he'd take it from me, so I'd focus on him. But I still wasn't really present. The worst was the complete lack of intimacy and connection during sex. He knew I wasn't present and just going through the motions. He knew I was engaging in it out of obligation, just being nice to him. And he always knew when I was faking an orgasm just to move things forward so it would be done, and I could go back to checking out.

Sex was way too much effort when I hated myself that much. There was no way I'd give myself permission to experience the pleasure of orgasm or connection because I felt unworthy. I didn't love myself, so why would anyone else? If I reject him first and keep him at a distance by being an asshole, he won't see how sad and broken I am inside. The problem was, HE ALWAYS KNEW! Even though he could see and feel the pain I was in, what I was doing and who I was being left him hurt and rejected.

BUSINESS

Recently, writing this book has been a huge trigger for all my old bullshit stories of not enough and unworthy. To be completely honest, writing this book has been the biggest sabotage trigger I've had in a very long time. Talk about pushing outside the comfort zone and embracing my truth and authenticity. This is scary as hell! And the result has been resistance, avoidance, distraction, and even emotional eating.

In fact, I wrote this chapter last—yes after the rest of the book was done—as I'm living the sabotage and writing about it at the same time. Sharing this much of my truth and vulnerability has stirred up my inner critic and sabotage in different ways. Worrying about it being good enough, I found myself moving the stories around a bunch of times to find the "perfect" fit. I've noticed my deep fear of rejection creeping up. Not the readers rejecting it, but those I'm closest to that I include in my stories, like my husband and parents.

Then the visibility blocks pop up from that place of worthiness, like "who are you to write a book?"—a throwback from being taught not to shine too brightly as it makes others uncomfortable, which is a lot of pressure as a kid, to be responsible for the feelings of others.

What's been most challenging is digging into my past and allowing myself to be present with the experiences and emotions I'm bringing up for this book. Being totally honest with myself about who I was during my worst times. Being an observer to my childhood traumas and sharing those stories with you. It's really brought up a lot of emotion, but also an immense amount of clarity and understanding. I've been able to connect even deeper to my truth and understand my past in a more profound way than ever before, learning to embrace more of my story and love myself in a greater capacity. And it just keeps growing.

SYMPTOMS

Your sabotage happens in cycles. You experience levels of high productivity and success, then avoidance, distraction, excuses, shut down, or all of the above. You take action, which triggers your critic, which fuels self-doubt and inaction. Some of your sabotage cycles may be hours or days, while other cycles are months or even years before you're able to get back on track and move forward. Either way, during sabotage you're STUCK. Your primary form of sabotage is control issues: perfection, procrastination, expectation, assumption, dishonesty, and judgment. When in full effect, control issues lead to other forms of sabotage, like avoidance, distraction, and excuses. Overall, control is curating the version of you that you're sharing with the world and attempting to control how others perceive, think, and feel about you.

PERFECTION

Perfection is controlling who you're being and the quality of your performance in some area to mask your underlying feelings of unworthy and not good enough. It's chronically striving for the unattainable, which reinforces your belief that you're not good enough. Procrastination falls under this heading as well because it's actually a perfectionist problem. Either you don't have the perfect situation to start a task or project (you don't have the perfect amount of time, space, energy, resources, etc. to start). Or you don't feel like what you're doing is good enough, i.e. PERFECT ENOUGH, to call it finished. You expend so much energy in trying to be perfect that you're exhausted and burned out.

EXPECTATION

Expectation is the biggest control issue of our inner critic, as well as the most prevalent control issue as it leads to the others. Expectation is trying to control things in your head. If you expect a bad outcome from something you're doing, you procrastinate finishing it or keep working to make it perfect, fueling worry, doubt, and your inner critic. You become trapped in external expectations about who you *should* be or how you *should* build a business. We waste energy curating ourselves into this false identity based on *shoulds* and disconnecting from the truth of who we are.

If you're living a life based on expectation, you're giving your power away to external conditions. Giving away control over yourself and your life leads to feeling out of control inside. That's the discontent and disconnect we feel, a prevailing sense of powerlessness that fuels our victim perspective.

A victim reacts or responds to what happens to them, feeling as though circumstances are outside of their control. If the beliefs of your wounded inner child are running your life, of course, you're functioning with a victim perspective. Children don't have any control over themselves or their lives. When feeling that out of control and powerless, the dominant symptoms are control issues because you want to feel in control of something.

WORRY

Worrying about what others think about you is perhaps one of the most crippling ways in which we give our power away to the expectations of others. It is one of the earliest steps in the sabotage cycle that leads to all the other forms of sabotage. We have an idea of who we think we *should* be to avoid rejection from others and get their approval. Basically, we expect rejection if we are our real, authentic selves, so, we curate and control who we are and how we present ourselves to control how others perceive us, what they think and feel about us, to avoid rejection.

SOURCE

The root of your sabotage is the belief that you're not good enough to be successful. That's why your sabotage is in cycles. As mentioned in the book *The Big Leap* by Gay Hendricks, your comfort zone is like a thermostat setting, for example preferring between 72–74 degrees. Anything below that setting generates discomfort, so you work hard to get yourself back up to your comfort zone setting. But anything above the upper limit of your ideal setting means you'll sabotage the shit out of your life and business to come back down to what's comfortable. He calls it an Upper Limit problem. Right now, all the work you're doing to get your goals is interfering with your upper limit because your entire comfort zone is below your goals.

When you've sabotaged yourself enough that you're below the lower limit, you focus and hustle yourself into some amazing success, often with great ease. But that momentum will quickly take you past your upper limit, and that's when the sabotage cycle starts all over again. The upper limit is where you're hitting against your limiting belief that you are not good enough for that level of success, joy, good stuff, ease and flow, health, or connection. Or any other resource for that matter. Your inner critic and sabotage are the resistance you create to get yourself below the upper limit quickly and back to feeling comfortable. What I share with you throughout this book aids in aligning with your authentic self to adjust your upper limit.

EGO

Your ego is all about separation rather than connection. It focuses on all the things that will keep you safe and small. It's the filter that helps you see only what is wrong or bad with you so you continue to believe that you're not enough. And in the process, you disconnect from your true self (and Source) and from others out of fear. Always worrying what other people think, functioning in a defensive space (victim mode), thinking somehow people are always judging you. But the reality is, you aren't that important in the lives of others in terms of them worrying about what you're doing or not doing. Most people are too busy, too wrapped up in their own lives to worry to the degree you think they are about what you're doing. As I've mentioned, in the separateness of our ego, we judge others, but that is just a reflection of our self-judgment.

INNER REBEL

Your inner rebel is the source of your impulsive, often reckless behavior that causes trouble. Often you just feel compelled to be bad for the sake of being bad, breaking free from the expectation of who you think you *should* be. However, the inner rebel can be some of our strongest sabotage when we had plans to do something goal-oriented and instead, we do absolutely NOTHING. Or the rebel is the wild child or partier that leads to eating or drinking too much, even acting out to cope with your emotions. But the rebel is just part of your authentic self that becomes powerful enough to escape through the curated version of you.

The more disconnected and out of alignment you are from your true, authentic self, being this fake version of who you think you *should* be, the more your truth works to break free and be expressed. Your authentic self isn't inherently a rebel; however, your authentic self isn't keen on going with the grain or following what everyone else is doing. And the more you ignore your truth, the more often it will show up in destructive ways, rather than constructive ways.

SOLUTION

Even though it seems like you're completely future-focused with your sabotage, it's the overwhelming emotional baggage from your past that fuels the worry, what ifs, and expectation. Your ego is filtering your personal history to focus on evidence that supports your limiting beliefs to predict future outcomes. And your authentic self is screaming to be included in your life.

The first thing to keep in mind is that we are not working to eliminate sabotage, only shorten your sabotage cycles. As you move forward, growing and changing, it's like you're experiencing things for the first time ever. Plus, a more authentic (and a bit more vulnerable) you is near the surface, so you're still going to get triggered and sometimes still slide into sabotage cycles. The key is to recognize what's happening and effectively use the tools I share throughout this book to speed up your cycles, reducing them to days, hours, or even seconds for you to learn the lessons, get back on track, and move forward.

The way to reduce sabotage is to build a strong connection with you. The REAL, AUTHENTIC you! The more you learn to love and embrace your truth, the more you take your power back and take control of you. The more connected you are to YOU, the more you feel and believe that you're GOOD ENOUGH to be successful. The more you believe you're enough, the less you sabotage yourself, consequently eliminating or reducing your sabotage cycles. By connecting to you and nurturing that relationship, you adjust your upper limit by shifting your comfort zone to a higher level that aligns with your goals. This allows your success to be easier as you're no longer creating resistance and blocking yourself from being your best self or manifesting your dreams.

PERMISSION

A huge chunk of sabotage is just not giving yourself permission to be you or engage is pleasure, fun, or rest. If your inner rebel is being bad and sabotaging you, then giving yourself permission changes everything. Much of your sabotage comes from not listening to what your soul is telling you to do. You're working too much, not having fun, or just doing things that you're not passionate about. By giving yourself permission to have a day off, a snack or meal you're craving, doing something fun, or simply doing some self-care, you're able to alleviate a lot of the acting out and sabotage associated with this aspect of your disconnect from self. Ultimately, this is about giving yourself permission to be you.

EMPOWERED ACTION

RESOURCE

Utilize the Empowered Overthinker Method discussed in Chapter 9.

EXERCISE

- Identify where in your life or business you've been sabotaging yourself.

- How have you been sabotaging yourself?

    o Excuses, avoidance, distraction, numbing out, prep purgatory, etc.

JOURNAL

Where can you give yourself permission to be yourself?

CONNECT

Share your biggest discoveries and insights in the Facebook group from the resource, exercise, and journaling.

NOTES

_____

_____

_____

_____

_____

_____

_____

_____

_____

_____

_____

_____

CHAPTER 3: FOUNDATION FOR SUCCESS

PERSONAL

Throughout my life, people would always compliment me on my successes and achievement, acknowledging my accomplishments, how I did something, or appreciating my help. However, I generally laughed it off because I never saw what they did. My perception of myself was very distorted as I only saw what wasn't right, perfect, or good enough. I never felt like I was put together, organized, or presented myself well. I had such a negative filter on how I perceived myself and anything I did. In fact, most of the time I felt like a huge impostor because what they saw was not a reflection of the real me, just a curated façade. Plus, I wasn't seeing any of the good stuff they saw in me. This fueled the fear that I could never meet the expectation of who they thought I was. I was an impostor, posing as a successful person but a complete failure and wreck inside.

I remember one day when a friend complimented me, she told me that she admired how organized I was and how I always was so well put together. Inside I thought, "Boy, do I have you fooled. I'm a complete disaster!" For once, I managed to just smile and say "thank you" without deflecting or diminishing the compliment, which was uncommon, but this just made me feel like more of an impostor. How could I accept a compliment for something that wasn't true?

The disconnect came from the fact that I was faking my way through life. Looking pulled together and organized was one of the ways I hid the fact that I was falling apart inside. I felt unstable and out of control, so my control issues kicked in, and I showed up with a smile. The mask I wore kept people on the far outside of me, only seeing what I wanted them to see: the high-achiever who had her shit together and was always there with kindness or a helping hand. Yes, I was an achiever, but I was so disconnected from my truth that everything about me felt like a lie.

BUSINESS

I started my business from nothing more than an idea of what I thought it could be or perhaps *should* be. However, starting a business was a never-ending series of triggers to my sabotage and poor coping. Almost immediately, I was battling my inner critic, perfection, procrastination, and distraction. The biggest problem was not giving myself a clear direction or crafting a plan, so I would just hyper-focus on something that interested me, like building my website or a sales funnel, rather than doing revenue-generating activities. Honestly, not having a solid foundation for managing myself meant I didn't bother building a solid foundation for my business.

Even my decision to get certified as a health coach was based on a *should*. Because of my powerful health transformation, I *should* help people get healthy. Showing my dramatic before and after photos was an easy sell, rather than connecting to my truth and understanding what I was most passionate about when it came to helping others.

Because of these issues, my first year in business was a major struggle. I was out there flapping in the wind because I was building a business in pieces, trying a bunch of different things without a foundation or a clear plan. I had no clarity on why I was an entrepreneur other than the scarcity-driven motivation to become financially free. So, I grabbed at everything I could find and became a FREEBIE CHASER!

I downloaded every free guide, checklist, worksheet, and strategy pack. I enrolled in every webinar, masterclass, and challenge I saw that seemed to address what I thought were the problems in my business. There were two problems with this: 1) it kept me really busy in analysis paralysis, never doing any revenue-generating activities or building confidence by actually coaching people; 2) they only addressed the symptoms, never the real problem, which was me getting in my own way.

But the first year all my business did was cost me money that I didn't have. I was running it with no plan or foundation, fueling sabotage cycles and feeling stuck . . . and ended up creating more debt. The biggest problem was that I felt like I had to do it all on my own. This left me exhausted and burned out, feeling like my business was running me rather than me running my business. I was constantly hustling because I was desperate to make my business work and prove myself.

SYMPTOMS

Your current foundation is built on the coping skills and habits you learned early in life from your family of origin. Some people have a strong foundation that can withstand any storm. Others, like us, have a poorly built foundation with pieces missing, holes and patches, or made from insufficient materials to get your goals and be your best self. You feel unstable and out of control, so you distract yourself with the futile efforts of trying to control things that are not within your control, but that makes it worse. It doesn't take much for you to crumble or fall into cycles of self-doubt, sabotage, inconsistency, and instability. Leaving you overwhelmed, exhausted and reacting to everything rather than being proactive. You're not able to show up as your best.

Lacking a solid foundation is like building an empire on a game of Jenga: it's unstable and ready to fall at any moment. Then it becomes the story of the Dutch boy with his finger in the levee. Even though things are crumbling around you and all the negativity and fear is leaking out of the poor foundation, you try to patch and prevent leaks. You attempt to mask the problem by hiding behind control issues and achievement, you downplay the problem with sabotage and distraction, you hide behind a smile, faking it and pretending you're okay when you are far from it. So, we experience the inner critic and sabotage problems discussed in the previous chapters.

IMPOSTOR SYNDROME

In fact, the mask we wear is one of the heaviest burdens we carry. The lack of stability from a poorly built foundation leaves you constantly scrambling to feel in control of something because we're so out of control. So, you focus all your energy on looking the part, curating an image of who you think you *should* be or who will be approved by those around us. Basically, pretending to be somebody you're not hides the fact that you're falling apart inside. You end up exhausted and overwhelmed because you're compensating for not feeling good enough, so you over give, overcommit, overdeliver, and undercharge to counter your limiting beliefs, fear, lack, and insecurities.

The flipside to that is not seeing the good you do, so when you are genuinely complimented for your successes, you still feel like an impostor because there's no way you could live up to the version of you they have in their head. It's a catch 22 situation.

SOURCE

YOUR TOOLKIT

The foundation I'm referring to is your toolkit, which consists of the coping skills, mindset, beliefs, and habits that you've developed over the course of your lifetime. You're not born with a toolkit, it's learned from your family of origin, the bulk of which occurs before the age of seven. That's why much of your current toolkit still carries family patterns and generational traumas that you learned early in life. For the most part, your family is unaware of what they were passing on to you (and still engaging in today; that's why they're so frustrating).

When your toolkit lacks what you need to reach your goals or be your best, it means you don't have a solid foundation. This is why you're struggling with self-doubt and your inner critic—the tools you have are hindering rather than helping. For example, my toolkit was missing important effective coping skills to deal with hurt and rejection. Rather than talking to someone close to me about my feelings or journaling to understand, I was taught to stuff my feelings with food and avoid my emotions with distraction. This is a coping skill, just an unhealthy one. So, the tools in my toolkit were effective in the short-term but caused major problems for me long-term.

This isn't about judging the toolkit you have or those you learned it from. Honor yourself and your current toolkit because it's gotten you here, right now! You've recognized what's not serving you, that you need to learn some new skills to be your best self, and you're reading this because you're ready to change!

When your toolkit lacks the effective tools to help you be your best, that poor foundation leads you to feel unstable and ungrounded. Think about the Jenga example. Teetering and shaking as you build upward leaves you feeling unsteady and out of control. This poor foundation fuels many of the control issues and the curated façade we present to others. In fact, being who we think others expect us to be is part of our toolkit to hide our unstable foundation. But this instability leads to fear, scarcity, and feeling out of control.

Many of the choices we make are driven by the fear of losing the safety and stability we've created in our lives, but the stability is external and, therefore, doesn't fix the problem. The instability comes from within, and no external condition will solve the problem. This is why we make choices based on maintaining safety and stability, like not quitting our day job to commit to our own business, staying because of benefits, staying in unhealthy relationships long after we needed to leave, not growing your business or taking action to get your goals. All of those things would trigger a lack of safety and stability because you're outside your comfort zone. The need for safety and stability will trump motivation and goals every time.

COMPARTMENTALIZING

The other component to lacking stability in your foundation is that you put holes there yourself by compartmentalizing and by editing out the hurts and history you don't want to accept, the things you don't love about yourself, the anger and resentment you won't let go of, and all the stuff you're not being honest with yourself about. We lock away those experiences, hurts, failures, rejections, losses, and things we just plain hate about ourselves. We separate them from the person we present to the world, deep down in little compartments within ourselves, walled off, hoping they never come to the surface or anyone finds out about our darkness, our shadow self. This is the starting point for much of our self-rejection.

But that darkness leaks out as random ruminating thoughts that pop up in the quiet time, like when you're driving alone or falling asleep, or when your inner rebel is acting out. Those are the thoughts and feelings we distract ourselves from by staying busy or checking out on social media. It's why we avoid being quiet and alone with ourselves, so we don't have to FEEL it.

Like it or not, all that stuff is a part of you, even if you ignore it. The more you push the pain and darkness away, attempting to edit it out of yourself, the more inauthentic you feel. You're not WHOLE when you remove parts of you from you. You feel the void and then fill it with busyness, people, food, alcohol, distraction, exercise, anything that will help you avoid connecting to the truth of who you are, darkness and all. That's where your truth lies: through the personal history you're pretending didn't happen, the thoughts and feelings you feel guilt and shame for having, through the anger and resentment.

The only way to build a solid, stable foundation is to lean into all of it. But the key is to do it in a constructive, rather than destructive, way. A way that is safe and effective. Your full power lies in embracing your darkness and pain, not just the light of you. It's what helps you be empathetic and understanding, deeply connecting to others. It's the darkness that allows you to shine brightly since it's the source of your greatest strength.

SOLUTION

FOUNDATION

Success really is built on a solid foundation. You're reading this book because your foundation is challenged. As a high-achiever and perfectionist myself, I've always preferred to jump to step 27 before completing steps 2, 3, and 4. If your foundation is built upon unhealthy family patterns, generational traumas, personal trauma or instability, failure, limiting beliefs, disconnect and doubt, then the evidence will show as the symptoms discussed throughout this book manifest. The holes and cracks start to show because it's built with poor quality materials. Keep in mind, this analogy helps paint a picture of what you're doing with this book. You're going into your foundation, addressing the root issues compromising the integrity, restructuring and building a new foundation. You'll dig up and clear out the junk, patch holes and weak spots, and create a strong base to build the life and business of your dreams.

The most important component to your foundation is a strong connection to YOU. That's it. But it's everything. That connection is the source of your confidence, your authenticity, your aligned goals, and action. This is the path to embracing ALL of you and loving yourself as whole, no more compartmentalizing. That connection is built through self-management, learning to take control of you and no longer wasting time, energy, and emotion on things outside of your control. You must take your power back to build that connection.

The process of taking your power back and building your foundation for success is by implementing the foundational 5 Rs for success in my Aligned Abundance Process™. It's called the "Aligned Abundance Process" because it takes you through building a strong connection to you by aligning with your truth. The more fullness and enoughness you feel in that place of alignment, which is the source of feeling abundant, the more abundance you attract into your life and business. Every step will be thoroughly explained in each of the next five chapters.

ALIGNED ABUNDANCE PROCESS

ANCHOR YOUR ROUTINES – Doing consistent daily actions to show up for you, build a connection to you, and be your best to get your goals.

RELEASE YOUR BAGGAGE – Releasing the thoughts, emotions, and bullshit stories that keep us reactive, and letting go of things that are not within our control.

RESPECT YOUR BOUNDARIES – Taking responsibility for yourself and what you want to create, as well as creating safety and stability from within.

BE OPEN TO RECEIVE – Finally giving yourself permission to be successful and allowing all the abundance in that you're currently working too hard to create and attract.

RAISE YOUR STANDARDS – Upgrading and elevating how you show up, what you use, and who you surround yourself with to consistently be your best.

EMPOWERED ACTION

RESOURCE

Refer to the resources shared in the next five chapters to support each step in the Aligned Abundance Process.

EXERCISE

What habits and coping methods no longer serve you?

JOURNAL

- What about your life doesn't feel safe or stable?
- Identify how you've been hiding behind a mask or façade?

CONNECT

Share your biggest discoveries and insights in the Facebook group from what you learned in this chapter, the exercise, and journaling.

NOTES

_____

_____

_____

CHAPTER 4: ANCHOR YOUR ROUTINES

PERSONAL

Growing up, I saw a disconnect between structure and expectation. My mom is a creative at heart, a free spirit, so I had very little structure outside of getting ready for school, going, and coming home. Sleep was the only semi-consistent routine for me: I often went to bed and got up at the same time during the week. But the weekends were free game, and during the summer or if my mom wanted to do something together, my sleep schedule would vary. There was very little structure to support the expectation they had for me with regard to cleaning my room, doing homework, or doing chores. So most of the time, I never did those things, pushing them off and procrastinating until I HAD to do them because of consequences.

Basically, I lacked *responsibility* for my time and following through with tasks. This carried through in all aspects of my life, long before I started a business. It affected my grades in school because I wasn't consistent with doing my homework, despite easily getting "A's" as an overachiever. My lack of routine and consistency contributed to my health and weight issues because I never had a plan or routine for meals or exercise. When I was in the Army, life was easier because my routine was given to me. Plus, any corporate job I had, all my tasks or routines were dictated by someone else. But, stepping up and being responsible for my time and focus anywhere else in my life was a huge challenge. Basically, if I can put something off until I have to do it, I will. I procrastinate until pressure and panic force me to get it done.

BUSINESS

The same problems showed up when I started my business. Of course, my expectation was consistent growth and success, but I had no structure, systems, or routines to support that goal. I had NO CONSISTENCY whatsoever! Social media posting was random, Facebook Lives were even more sparse, emails were nonexistent, and I never seemed to have a plan for what I was going to do. There was no focus to my day, in fact, my days were really out of control. So, the "office day" that I intended to be super productive, would completely slip away from me. I'd be exhausted at the end of the day because I was super "busy" doing a bunch of prep tasks or distraction items, but never focused on revenue-generating activities.

Not having a clear routine was why I often stayed in preparation purgatory, with no plan or direction. Often forgetting about my goals and just getting sucked down the rabbit hole of creating a flyer or a landing page in my funnel. A lot of getting ready without ever actually doing the specific tasks that would get me closer to my goal. This lack of direction amplified my control issues because I constantly felt out of control. I didn't have any control over my time or my business growth. Because I was distracted and busy doing little things, I procrastinated in completing beneficial tasks like creating a list-building free offer or following up with potential clients. This was procrastination at an unconscious level because I simply had no clue where to focus my time, energy, and attention.

SYMPTOMS

The primary symptom of lacking a routine is procrastination or no follow-through. You're never doing what you intend to do for yourself or your business. A lot of action and energy is expended with little results to show for it. Or you simply never reach your goals.

UNFOCUSED

You're unfocused, with your time and energy flying all over the place. It's like the spray and pray method. Spray energy everywhere into a bunch of things and pray your business does well. When lacking focus and direction, it's easy to get caught up in distraction. If you time block two hours for business building activities, but end up doing laundry, talking to your friend for 45 minutes, checking social media, and getting sucked down the scroll hole, by the end, you've only spent a total of 10 minutes working on your business and worn yourself out doing a bunch of other stuff. But you're frustrated why you're two hours of "business time" isn't generating results or revenue in your business.

Lots of people think they have ADD and focus issues, but really, they're lacking a plan for their time and not making ANY time for themselves. So, you get sucked into distraction because you feel the need to be busy or you're distracted because you just can't focus on work anymore. You're not giving yourself any time to disconnect from work or life, so focusing on anything becomes difficult.

Another symptom when you're lacking focus is taking on too many other things for other people. You're not clearly committed enough to specific tasks to say "no" to other things. Think about your excuses for not getting things done. Most excuses are totally justifiable. Not following up with clients because your kid got sick. Their game ran late, so you didn't send that email. Other people and tasks that require energy and attention are taking priority, so there's little energy left to focus on you or your goals. Then, you're not setting aside time after the excuses to handle what MUST be done for your business to succeed. You see the excuse as a permanent thing, instead of a slight delay. You're not committing to what needs to be done enough for delays or excuses not to stop you from following through. Allowing justifiable excuses to interfere with getting your goals is one of the most common forms of sabotage.

EXHAUSTION

You simply cannot focus your time or energy on reaching your goals when you're exhausted. All the overworking and busyness drain you of energy, and a lack of return on your time investment leaves you feeling even more disappointed and critical of yourself. Spending a lot of time and energy on the wrong things is why we experience business burnout. Think about how exhausting it is when you're overthinking, analyzing, and worrying, working really hard but never seeing a return on your investment. However, a lot of your busyness is being busy for the sake of doing something, as your old beliefs equate busyness to value and worth. The busyness is another form of external validation to prove ourselves.

NO FOLLOW-THROUGH

You feel like your to-do list keeps getting longer and longer (with all the things you *should* be doing) but not much ever gets done. This is more than procrastination; you simply don't have systems or strategies in place to follow through with any regularity. Then, there are the tasks you label in your mind as "difficult": you don't know how to do them, they require a large amount of time or energy, or they seem draining. So those tasks stay on the list because you continue to avoid getting them done.

SOURCE

RESISTANCE

Lots of high-achievers hate the idea of structure, wanting to work when in the flow or feeling inspired, but your inner critic and control issues are fueled by feeling out of control. Not following through or being consistent with your goals or business are signs of sabotage. In fact, your inner rebel is the part of you that is resistant to structure and routine, craving freedom but instead contributing to feeling unfocused and out of control. But the truth is, we thrive in consistency! The key is creating a balance between nurturing your inner rebel (which is a good thing) and quieting your inner critic. A solid routine helps you to feel in control, funneling time and energy into what's most important—you and your goals.

GUILT

Making your wellbeing the top priority over everything and everyone else makes you feel guilty. Even if you plan on self-care and doing things for you, something always seems to come up or get in the way. Or, if you actually do make time for you, you're not fully present, worrying about everyone else or just feeling guilty about making time for you. That's because you are the lowest priority on your list of priorities. More likely, you're not even ON your priority list.

REWARD

Let's talk about brain chemistry for a moment, as this impacts your ability to finish certain tasks. Upon the completion of a task, your brain gets a dopamine hit, giving you feelings of pleasure and satisfaction. This is huge for your motivation-reward cycle. Basically, it helps you to see the reward and take action to get there.

As an entrepreneur, your business as a whole never seems done, so there is not a specific completion reward. You're likely quite dopamine-starved right now, and that's why you're in the cycle of avoiding your business goals and other tasks that don't feel like they're ever complete. But where you *do* get a reward is in finishing things like the laundry or dishes. When it's done, you know it's complete and get a dopamine hit. This is a huge contributor to why your distraction is often centered on other types of busyness and completion. Finishing a landing page or flyer is much more rewarding to your brain than making calls or sending emails.

SOLUTION

IT'S ABOUT YOU

A successful routine focuses on nourishing you, grounding you for your day, and helping you stay on target with your goals. All the gurus are right...win your morning to win your day. Even if everything else falls apart, rocking your morning sets you up for success! Following a routine helps you feel in control of you because you're anchoring yourself in the morning. Keeping the bulk of this routine focused on nourishing YOU also builds your relationship with yourself. That connection to you is the foundation for confidence and key for eliminating the underlying limiting beliefs like not good enough or worthy.

You may be grumbling at the idea of a routine! *Been there, done that, doesn't work.* The problem is, most routines are focusing on the wrong things. Think about your current daily routine. I'll bet almost every task on the list is focusing on others or—if it is about you—it's very autopilot stuff...get up, brush teeth, get ready, wake kids, get the kids dressed and fed, pack lunches, do laundry, run this errand, make that call, etc. Other routines you've tried may have been addressing the symptoms, like the procrastination, by mapping out your tasks differently instead of addressing the underlying cause of your procrastination.

ACCOUNTABILITY

No matter how awesome your routine is, it needs to be consistent. We often see the result of not being consistent in our business when we're struggling to find leads, but it starts with being consistent with your routine. Consistency comes from tracking your routine! Tracking what you are and aren't doing with your routine is the personal accountability you need to make sure you're ACTUALLY doing what you plan. It's what ensures follow through and success. It doesn't matter how or where you track your routine: in your planner, to-do list, app, journal, or simple tracker just for your routine.

The idea of tracking can be anxiety-inducing because it's another way we fuel the inner critic. But we aren't using the tracker so that bitch in our head has more ammo to use against us. Tracking is for accountability and understanding your trends. That's it. This isn't about being PERFECT!

You don't need to have EVERY box checked for it to be a "good" day. Even if you do one thing for the day and it's at 3 pm, that's AWESOME...you did something! It's simply about understanding trends: what's working and what isn't. We can have wonderful intentions, but if we consistently avoid doing certain things and don't know it, it's hard to know what to change. Look for patterns over time. Are there specific things you're avoiding doing in your routine? This can highlight some subtle sabotage or underlying blocks that you may have not known about previously.

There are other benefits to tracking your routine. How you do one thing is how you do everything! So being consistent with your personal routine means more consistency elsewhere, like in your business. Plus, checking off your routine on the tracker gives you the dopamine hit! Then, you feel good! Having a paper or digital tracker is HUGE for maintaining motivation with your reward system, as well as knowing what's working and tracking your sabotage cycles. And, you build your tracking skills so you're more inclined to track data in other areas of your life and business, such as ROI, conversions, and finances.

YOUR ROUTINE

A morning routine is powerful and transformative when you're doing things that allow you to choose your energy, mindset, and intention for the day. You're practicing the skills of being present, feeling in control, and choosing how you will show up for the day. That little bit of structure and consistency creates feelings of stability and trust in yourself because you're learning to focus and be in control of you. Routines are about building a relationship with YOU, which is why they are so powerful for building confidence.

The morning—or whatever time you awaken for your day—is a great time to do your routine because you can make time for you before the day gets going. There are way too many excuses later in the day...we get busy or tired or something comes up. Knock this out before anyone else gets up. A simple evening routine is a great way to bookend the start and end of your day with time focused on you. If you ever have difficulty sleeping, having a PM routine that helps set your energy and mindset for bed is also powerful. These routines are a form of self-care because its time focused on you for you.

Some of the most powerful things I've done in my morning routine:

- **Gratitude** – This is the very first thing I do when I wake up! Stepping into a place of appreciation for all the blessings in your life and business right now allows you to create and attract more. The key when writing them down is to really FEEL it.

- **Journal** – I used to journal before bed but was often too tired to do it. Doing this in the morning has been a game-changer for consistency. Journaling gives you an opportunity to have a dialogue with yourself to understand your thoughts and feelings about the day.

- **Plan My Day** – This was one of the most beneficial steps to do in the morning so I knew how I'd be spending my day. I quickly review my schedule and carryover tasks from the day before. My paper planner is where I put the to-do list for today and organize errands or any other priorities for the day.

- **Action Step** – I write down a targeted action step that supports my top goal for the month. For example, if my goal is to enroll four new individual clients this month, an action step might be inviting a new contact to a call or following up with someone.

- **Other ideas to track with your routine:** exercise or stretching, using your vision board or doing a visualization, happy dancing (one of my favorites for a quick energy shift), declarations or affirmations, reading or devotional time, meditation or prayer. Anything that will raise your energetic vibration first thing and put you in a positive, uplifted mood.

- **Evening routine items:** gratitude, good things about today, my biggest success from today, reading or prayer. Of course, add any other items that help you see the good from your day and prepare you for happy, healthy sleep.

Add anything else to your routine that makes your heart sing.

START SIMPLE

The key is to start with a simple morning routine! Don't overwhelm yourself with TOO MUCH to start. It's okay to add one or two things you already do consistently to the list to help you feel good about starting this new habit. When I first started implementing a morning routine, mine consisted of making my bed and brushing my teeth. That's it. It was so soon after my rock bottom moment, that was all I could handle. A little self-care with personal hygiene and creating order in my space by making the bed. However, that small change was the catalyst to a very rapid and powerful transformation.

EMPOWERED ACTION

RESOURCE

Download the AM/PM Routine Tracker.

EXERCISE

- Create your daily routine and start doing it.

    o Start implementing your routine every day or every weekday and track your progress.

- Put your tracker up where you can see it first thing in the morning and just before bed.

- Be kind and patient with yourself as it takes time to implement new habits.

JOURNAL

Why have you resisted or struggled with routines in the past?

CONNECT

Ask questions in the Facebook group if you're struggling with creating your routine.

- Share your routine in the group for additional accountability.

NOTES

_____

_____

_____

_____

_____

_____

_____

_____

_____

_____

_____

_____

_____

CHAPTER 5: RELEASE YOUR BAGGAGE

PERSONAL

My husband would always tell me it wasn't what I said, but how I said it. It never sounded bad in my head, whatever it was, but by the time it came out of my mouth, it went through a filter of anger, resentment, and discontent. Everything was tainted with a shitty tone when it left my mouth. And everyone could feel that I wasn't "alright." I felt out of control inside, which fueled my control issues. The more out of control I felt inside, the more I numbed out and checked out, especially with food and alcohol. I was constantly STUFFING my emotions in one way or another.

When I was sober and not distracted with work or external drama, I would distract myself by trying to control things that didn't matter, like how my husband did the dishes. In fact, my husband and I both numbed out with food, alcohol, and television, so I know that being a control freak made numbing out worse too. The emotional baggage we both carried, along with my chronic control issues, nearly destroyed our marriage. I was constantly triggered and reacting to everything.

I had a negative filter pulled over my entire life during this time. Everything was either shitty or just never good enough. However, if something was going right, I had a fantastic ability to take a nice moment and ruin it by opening my mouth and saying something shitty. I used to pride myself on 'telling it like it is' or saying what everyone was thinking. But my honesty wasn't just honest, it was brutal honesty with an emphasis on "brutal." If I wasn't happy, I couldn't find it in myself to let others be happy.

This all happened at the subconscious level, too. I swear I wasn't an asshole on purpose (most of the time). That's just who I was: an asshole. It was a defense mechanism to keep people at a distance, so I didn't have to worry about being vulnerable and everyone seeing I was just a scared little girl inside, rejecting them before they could reject me. My inner rebel was lashing out in a destructive way to myself and others. Honestly, I could be outright mean! And I hated being that person.

BUSINESS

The first big month I had in my business was just over $5,000, which was a huge jump from the $1,000–$2,000 I had previously been attracting. Despite having big financial goals, this was a HUGE trigger because it jumped past my upper limit. It sent me into a tailspin of old habits and sabotage that lasted nearly 4 months. With this new uplevel in clients, I got even busier and worked even more, but all I was doing was avoiding my emotions around money and success. Not only did I avoid work, but I also started numbing out again with food and TV. Plus, it was summer, so I could justify my increased drinking as part of the summer picnic and holiday season. However, I didn't do any revenue-generating activities for months, so I had no income for months. Actually, I made nothing or lost money because I was subconsciously balancing out my previous success with struggle.

The worst part was that my filter of negativity resurfaced. But it was ALL directed toward me! I was an ASSHOLE to myself; nothing was right or good enough. However, it started to creep up at home, so my husband now received collateral damage from me getting emotionally backed up again. That was a HUGE indicator that I was not alright and feeling the pressure. That's where the negativity came from, this self-imposed pressure to be successful, to prove something, to not be a failure, to be a financial contributor to the household. And at the same time, I never felt good enough or worthy of the success I was working so hard to achieve.

SYMPTOMS

EMOTIONAL BURDEN

I'm sure you feel it, that HUGE emotional burden you're carrying. The baggage you're bringing with you from moment to moment, attempting to hide it away, but it leaks out when you get triggered and overreact! You worry that, at any moment, you could blow up and totally lose your shit! Basically, you're easily triggered by others, by you, by outcomes, by sabotage, by your critic, and just about anything else. It doesn't take much for you to lose control of your emotions and go down the rabbit hole of worry and fear or sabotage and negativity. In fact, dumping on others is the most common method of release, like picking a fight with your spouse or snapping at your kids. Or just breaking down and bawling your eyes out because you can't keep it together any longer.

Your emotional baggage likes to pop up at the worst times (like when you're feeling really good or focused). The guilt, anger, or judgment toward yourself because of what you're doing or who you're being right now, like saying "no" or still getting sucked into sabotage. Taking on the emotions of others but feeling more out of control and overwhelmed because they're not your responsibility. Crushed by the burden of responsibility you place on yourself to do all and be all for everyone all the time until you shut down. The expectations of yourself, your business, and others in your life.

OUT OF CONTROL

But you don't know what to do with your emotions or how to handle what you're feeling. All of this emotional overwhelm leads to feeling out of control inside, which triggers your control issues. Attempting to control things, outcomes, or people that you don't have control over makes you feel even more exhausted and out of control. When you don't know what to do with your emotions, the easiest thing is to numb out. That's how you cope. Stuffing your emotions with food or alcohol. Distracting yourself by focusing on taking care of your kids, helping others, or telling your partner all the things they're doing wrong. Avoiding your emotions by staying really busy and never being alone with YOU because then you'll actually FEEL it.

The more you avoid the emotions, the more they creep up at the worst times. This is why we ruminate, consciously or when we're not focused on something else, like when driving or falling asleep. This rumination fuels your guilt and shame, anger and resentment, so your inner critic gets worse and you feel terrible remembering old hurts and mistakes. Which keeps you in the same cycle of your emotional burden feeding your overwhelm, and you eventually blow up or shut down.

SOURCE

REACTION

When you're in a constant state of reaction, you cannot take action to get your goals. You cannot react and act at the same time. That's why being triggered leads to sabotage and inaction. Pushing outside your comfort zone triggers your old emotions. Doing what you think you *should* be doing rather than listening to your gut is triggering. Growing your business is triggering. Your kids and partner are triggering. Your inner critic triggers you even more because you're judging yourself for being triggered. It's a vicious cycle. The best visual representation I've ever seen of this cycle was by Kirk Duncan from 3 Key Elements. I've recreated a similar Reaction vs. Action graphic on the next page.

You are in the present moment, and something happens that triggers you. Your trigger is an experience or event that is attached to old emotions. A similar experience occurs or creates feelings in the present that have a direct link to those old emotions and experiences. Those old emotions are quickly brought into the present moment. Hence, your response is reactive. You are RE-ACTING out the old scenario in the present moment. That's why when you react to things, your response may seem out of context for the situation. Sometimes you can feel yourself being triggered and reacting. Other times, you're completely unaware as this cycle is playing out at a subconscious level, but you see the results of being triggered.

When you're taking action to create the future you want, you're bringing your goals closer to the present. You cannot take action toward your goals when you're in a state of reaction. You can only do one or the other. If you're constantly reacting, you aren't able to move forward, so you stay stuck living out your past in the present.

However, the more burden and baggage we're carrying around, the closer we are to the old emotions instead of taking action to get our goals. In fact, the closer we are to the past, the further we are from creating the life and business we want. It looks more like this:

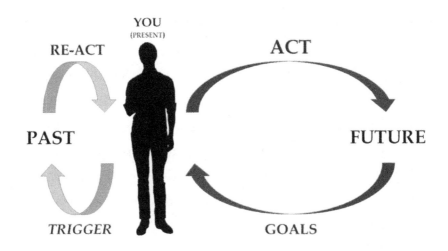

I lovingly call this emotional overwhelm being Emotionally Constipated! You're SO backed up with all this stuff you're taking on with nowhere for it to go. You don't have a constructive method of release. So, the emotion eventually leaks out. Something small happens, and you totally lose your shit. The kids get loud or spill something, and you snap at them. You pick a fight with your partner or dump on them just to let off some steam. Basically, dumping or crying are your only methods of release, or you stay bottled up until you explode.

SABOTAGE

Whenever I felt myself getting to that point, that's when I'd numb out. Food, alcohol, social media scroll hole, binging on TV. I'd use anything to distract from what I was feeling because I didn't know how to handle my emotions. All of that avoidance and lack of coping spilled over into sabotaging every aspect of my life and business.

The more out of control I felt inside, the more I tried to control things around me. That showed up in my business as expectation of outcome, procrastination with starting or completing projects, worrying about what others would think or say, or worrying about not being good enough or perfect enough. Not doing what I "should" do fueled my cycle of sabotage and self-judgment, which made me sabotage myself even more.

As I've mentioned, you learn your coping toolkit as a child, most of it developing between birth and age 7. Then we spend the rest of our life reinforcing those habits and beliefs. Your toolkit is comprised of generational patterns taught to us by our family of origin. When that toolkit isn't working, over time we begin to feel out of control. This starts the control issues. Combine that with a belief that you're not good enough and that performance equals worth, and you get the Perfectionist!

SOLUTION

CONSTRUCTIVE RELEASE

Constructive release is the path to reducing your triggers. By releasing the emotions attached to these past experiences, you effectively reduce or remove the trigger that was keeping the past so close to your present. Your triggers are a direct emotional connection to past experiences, and that's why the reaction time can be so quick. The more your past is held close to the present, the more you're wearing these triggers on the surface. This is why you're in a constant state of reacting, constantly being triggered by the smallest things, giving you a short fuse before blowing up.

Constructive release disconnects the trigger by removing the emotional attachment to the past experience and helps you learn lessons as well. It's hard to see the value of your past until you learn the lessons. The lessons are the value, but when we're blinded by the hurt, anger, guilt, and resentment, we're blinded by the emotions. Those emotions keep us trapped as a victim and unable to learn the lessons. Releasing the emotional attachment and learning the lessons helps reduce or dissolve the trigger completely and helps you break free from feeling like a victim of your past.

By severing the emotional attachment to your past traumas and learning those lessons, you're able to be more in the present, less reactive, and take action to move forward. The key is to be proactive to be less reactive. This means using the tools and resources I'm sharing with you consistently to alleviate the emotions before you're ready to explode. When I started using release techniques, it was part of my daily routine to remove decades of emotional constipation.

There are numerous release techniques available all over the internet, but I'll share the most powerful ones I've used to help people like us.

JOURNALING. In the process of writing down your thoughts and feelings about the day, you have an opportunity to not only build a dialogue with yourself about what you're feeling, but to also understand what's triggering you in the present and why you're triggered.

TAPPING (EFT). This is a powerful process to break free from the old stories and emotional attachments and replace them with new thoughts so you can move forward.

It involves tapping on acupressure points; acknowledging the thoughts, emotions, and beliefs keeping you stuck; and replacing them with new, empowering ones.

WRITE & BURN. Writing your negative thoughts and feelings without restriction and destroying the paper when done. Basically, dumping on paper instead of onto others. By writing, it gives you an opportunity to gain a greater understanding of where your triggers are coming from, learn the lessons, and effectively release the negative thoughts and feelings. This is one of my absolute favorites because there are variations to fit every situation and lifestyle.

PHYSICAL RELEASE. If you're so emotionally overwhelmed you can't write or talk because you're ready to explode, it's a great idea to burn off the physical energy before using another release technique. This can be exercise, going to an empty field to scream, stomp, and throw a tantrum, screaming into a pillow, punching a pillow or punching bag, even buying cheap dishes or glasses from the thrift store to throw and break in a dumpster. There are a TON of options for a physical release, but the key is to make sure you're safe and no one else is exposed to the release of your negative energy.

EMPOWERED ACTION

RESOURCE

Download the Release Technique and use the ideal variation for you. Try a few to find the best fit.

EXERCISE

Practice a forgiveness exercise when your critic kicks in.

- Say I FORGIVE YOU aloud. Repeat as necessary. Take it to the next level by looking in the mirror and saying I FORGIVE YOU.

- Ho'oponopono – Hawaiian Forgiveness Prayer

  o Repeat aloud: I'm sorry. I forgive you. Thank you. I love you.

JOURNAL

- Who do you need to forgive?
- What or who has been your biggest trigger recently?

CONNECT

Share your most profound discovery or win in the Facebook Group.

NOTES

BE A BOSS & FIRE THAT BITCH

_____

_____

_____

_____

_____

_____

_____

_____

_____

_____

_____

_____

_____

_____

CHAPTER 6: RESPECT YOUR BOUNDARIES

PERSONAL

Growing up, I learned to be the rescuer and fixer. I was the oldest child in an abusive, narcissistic household, so I was often protecting my siblings. Plus, there were lots of boundary issues on both sides of my family, so by watching everyone, I learned to take responsibility for the emotions of others, like their happiness, or to passive-aggressively manipulate them to get my way. This dysfunctional foundation, along with my abandonment and rejection issues, taught me to be very codependent in my intimate relationships. I always managed to attract a "project guy" who needed rescuing. As I was ready and willing to take responsibility for his life, I attracted men who were irresponsible in most or all aspects of their lives. In the beginning, it's great because I'm too focused on them to worry about any of my own issues or problems. However, over time, it becomes exhausting and draining constantly giving your power away to someone else's life and difficulties. I was constantly picking up the pieces from their mistakes or doing everything myself. In fact, that made the transition to wanting a "partner" difficult.

My husband, Jeffry, and I have been married for 16 years, and we've been through a lot of challenges over the years because of the boundary issues we both brought to the relationship. I definitely stepped into the rescuer role in this relationship at the beginning, but we were both walled off behind the emotional baggage from our respective childhood traumas. He was a huge giver as well, but with strings attached because he needed validation or appreciation.

I was the exact same way. It's how we both gave to feel better and fill our cup. His giving was great for the scared little girl inside of me who needed rescuing as well. We were both victims and rescuers at various times, but I ended up being the one who took responsibility for our relationship, our household, and our lives. I took responsibility for his problems and issues, helping him work through it in the beginning. Actually, it was our similar victim perspectives that fueled our rescuing of each other to feel better and why we connected as kindred spirits.

Over time, two big problems crept up. One, I eventually wanted a partner instead of a project, which is a difficult transition after years of giving my power away from lacking any boundaries. The other problem was I was making myself responsible for everything in his life, so I became a control freak about everything he did. The control issues flared because, ultimately, I don't have any control over him, so that made it worse because I felt out of control.

Eventually, as I began to fall apart, I couldn't manage the responsibility of the marriage or household. I couldn't even manage myself. So, Jeff stepped up as best he could at the time. Keep in mind, we're together today because he's an amazing partner and we're both working on ourselves to be better in the marriage. However, we went through some crazy shit to get to the place where we are today.

BUSINESS

When I met my client Lindsay, she was exhausted from working all the time. The biggest issue for her was ALWAYS being available to her clients. For her business to be successful, she believed she needed to immediately respond to a call, text, email, or message, otherwise she'd lose clients and her business would suffer. Deep down, she believed that her business success and her own value came from giving to others in an unrestricted way. It's what she was taught. That's a lot of self-imposed pressure, on top of the fact that she built an independent real estate firm from the ground up.

She'd answer her phone at all hours of the day or night. We jokingly said her phone was like another appendage to her body when we first started working together. She'd always have it face up during meetings and even during our sessions at the beginning, so she could see the notifications that came up on the screen. If it seemed important, she'd even take a call or respond to a message.

As she gained awareness and understanding of her boundary issues, and finally created clear and effective boundaries, the most noticeable change was her availability. She panicked when I first asked her to turn off her phone for an hour per day. The idea of not being available challenged her beliefs about both herself and her business. Over the course of working together, she blocked out more and more time that she was not available. This allowed her to be totally present for herself and her kids. She enjoyed spending time with her girls and the greater quality of time they spent together. Even more powerful was the time she spent with herself, being totally present at the gym or during self-care. A strong connection developed within her, blossoming into a level of confidence she'd never experienced before.

Her healthy boundaries extended to every aspect of her life, personally and professionally. But the biggest change was her boundaries with herself. By respecting her boundaries, she's learned to love herself in a way she never had before. Because she is now showing up in her life as her best self, who she is being in her life is very different. She's lost over 60 pounds so far, more weight that she's ever lost before because, for the first time, she's getting healthy for herself, not for some external reason like an event or another person. Lindsay loves the fact that she's being an even better mom to her girls because she's fully present with them. She's setting a powerful example of how to be your best and break unhealthy family patterns by teaching them her new skills.

The evidence has been apparent in her business as well, even with having limited availability, she achieved her five-year goal in year two of her business! She no longer struggles with fear, worry, and scarcity, attracting abundance in all areas of her life and business. All because she implemented the Aligned Abundance Process, she's aligned with her goals, connected to her authentic self, and showing up as her best.

SYMPTOMS

RESPONSIBILITY

Boundary issues are about your responsibility, either not taking responsibility for what's yours or taking responsibility for what's not yours. You see these challenges in every relationship in your life, the relationship with yourself, others, time, money, your body, food, success, or other resources like health, joy, love, or support. If it's emotionally driven, it's a relationship.

When you're not taking responsibility for yourself, you're not responsible with resources, like time, money, food, and your body. When you're not responsible with your time, your schedule is out of control—there's no time for you or anything extra (but, people still ask you to do things). Feeling so out of control causes you to be inconsistent with following through with tasks or finishing things. The same thing happens with money, especially in your business. You're all over the place financially, feast or famine in your business, or your business may be costing you money. Or you simply have no idea where your money is actually going and don't stick to a budget.

The most common symptoms of boundary problems in relationships with others are one-sided or draining relationships. This is where you're taking responsibility for another person's life. We do this with partners, parents, and children the most by not allowing them to experience the consequences of their choices or behavior or making yourself responsible for their happiness, which ultimately you have no control over. That is their choice. This is the burden of the codependent, often taking responsibility for fixing another's life and rescuing them from their problems. You're effectively removing the effect of consequences for their actions and doing them a disservice by depriving them of their own life lessons. This is huge for parents "protecting" their children, but they are really just enabling them to not have to be responsible for themselves.

GUILT

Guilt is interesting because this is where we take emotional responsibility for stuff that isn't ours, adding to the emotional burden we carry. As Tony Robbins says, *We all experience pain, but suffering is a choice.* Guilt is one of our favorite flavors of suffering. Guilt comes from not being the person you think you *should* be, from not being able to make others happy, from not listening to your gut and living your truth, from not speaking up, and when you *do* speak up. Guilt is a double-edged sword because you're damned if you do and damned if you don't.

Think about how hard it is to say "no" when someone asks you for something. If you say "no" because you're doing something else, especially if it's for you or your business, you feel guilty. If you say "yes" to them, you feel guilty for not doing what you planned in the first place. In fact, we often don't say "no" because of responsibility. We feel responsible for doing things for others because we want them to be happy, which is just the mask for fearing rejection.

SOURCE

Nearly all the struggles and challenges you see in your life and business are NOT the problem. They are all just symptoms of the REAL ISSUE which is a lack of boundaries. The reason we keep struggling with those symptoms is that we usually focus on the symptom and not the root. Ultimately, we may experience improvement for a short time, but until we fix the boundary problems, all those challenges will eventually resurface.

We aren't born with boundaries, they are taught by our family of origin and developed in childhood as part of your toolkit. Those key people taught us the family patterns for navigating relationships, so we end up with the same types of boundary issues as those we grew up around. Because our parents or caretakers were unaware of their boundary problems, they shaped and molded our behavior and beliefs to reflect theirs. Even the healthiest and happiest childhoods can still create boundary problems if either parent had boundary problems. But, if you grew up with trauma, instability, addiction, abuse, or an absent or narcissistic parent, you probably recognize that you have some boundary problems.

FEAR

At the root, fear and limiting beliefs lead to our lack of boundaries. We fear rejection, abandonment or disapproval because we need validation or approval to feel like we're good enough. We believe we're not good enough, worthy, or deserving of boundaries because we lack confidence or a connection to ourselves. Everything in our lives becomes conditional. We need specific external conditions to fill the void of not good enough—conditions like someone approving of you or achieving success to feel better or enough. However, this is giving your power away to everything and everyone else! It's why we so often feel powerless and out of control, which triggers even more control issues and sabotage. And it's hard to feel confident when you're not in control of you. How you feel and who you're being is dictated by those external conditions. That's what has power over you.

GIVING YOUR POWER AWAY

Lacking boundaries means we're giving our power away! You give your power away because you're making other things or people responsible for how you feel and who you're being. You are responsible for YOU. The reason it seems so difficult is that you must get really honest with yourself about your wants and needs, something we tend to avoid. Also, if we've spent a lifetime giving away our power, we are not skilled in taking ownership or responsibility for ourselves. We give our power away by being responsible for things or other people that are not within our control. We give our power away by making outcomes or others responsible for what is actually ours, like our happiness or success.

Most people think about boundaries when discussing relationships with other people; however, you have a multitude of relationships in which boundaries apply. Many of the resources in which we struggle with scarcity, like time or money, are due to a strained relationship with that resource. Money and time can trigger very strong emotions, as well as other resources like joy, health, support, safety, and stability. How you manage resources like time or money is based on your boundaries. Basically, how responsible are you for managing that resource?

When we lack healthy personal boundaries, we create walls to protect ourselves. We use this method when our coping skills are limited by what we're taught as children. Walls work to a certain extent: it's why we have them for so long. However, I'll discuss more of the problems walls lead to in the next chapter. Walls stop some bad from getting in, but they also stop the good from getting in.

An even bigger problem is that our walls stop us from getting out, which leads to disconnect and feeling inauthentic. Because we've created walls around certain parts of us, compartmentalizing our past and emotions, we're walled off and disconnected from ourselves. To safely dismantle those walls, we must have another method of protection in the place first, which are our boundaries.

SOLUTION

Boundaries are limits and standards for what you will and will not allow. They are also a delineation between you and others, where you end and others begin. They are a powerful tool for protecting your energy, emotion, and physical space. Responsibility is the simplest explanation for what boundaries are—what you are or are not responsible for. You are responsible for what you will and will not allow. You are responsible for YOU—your thoughts, feelings, beliefs, and actions. You are NOT responsible for the thoughts, feelings, beliefs, or actions of anyone else. You are not responsible for things that are outside of your control.

The most profound shift you can make with responsibility is identifying what you actually have control over and what you don't. What you don't have control over is NOT your responsibility.

THE MIRROR EFFECT

We see the challenges and struggles in our external relationships with both people and resources. However, every single relationship you have is a mirror reflection of the one you have with yourself, which means the boundary problems you have in those relationships reflect the boundary problems with yourself. If you have people in your life that don't respect your time, energy, or wisdom, that's because you don't respect your time, energy, or wisdom. **Therefore, everything starts with your relationship with you.** You set the example for others as to how you are to be treated, what you will and will not allow. It's impossible to expect respect from someone else when you don't respect yourself. If you don't respect your own time, why would someone else?

This is why the process of building and holding to your boundaries is so important to boosting confidence. You're setting the example for every relationship because you're connecting to the truth of who you are, being honest, and taking responsibility for yourself to have clear and effective boundaries. In learning to trust yourself, you're building a strong connection with you, which is the foundation of confidence.

THE POWER OF "NO"

The boundaries we create for external relationships also apply to your relationship with YOU. ALL your relationships, with people and with resources, are ultimately just a reflection of the relationship you have with YOURSELF. If you aren't responsible with your time or money, that's due to a lack of boundaries with yourself. All your boundaries are about YOU, your internal "no." Being able to say "no" to old habits, unhealthy situations, things that don't serve you, people who are toxic or draining, or sabotage cycles means you can say "yes" to your goals and being the best you.

When our internal "no" is weak, we sabotage ourselves or buy into excuses, and then beat ourselves up, making us even more powerless. Boundaries with yourself and strengthening your internal NO is your key to consistency and follow through and, of course, channeling your inner rebel in a constructive way rather than destructive.

What does a boundary look like?

The most important and fundamental boundary you can have is NO DISRESPECT. Clear, strong language gets clear, strong results. This specific boundary applies to everything—no disrespect of my time, body, energy, wisdom, emotions, etc. What you're projecting with your energy is *I do not allow myself to be disrespected.*

As I mentioned, this boundary applies to the relationship with yourself, as we disrespect ourselves the most by what we say and do. Of course, when it comes to other people, we can't control what they say or do, but we do control how we respond. We set the example for how others are allowed to treat us by how we treat ourselves. Honoring your boundary and treating yourself with respect teaches others how to treat you. Respecting yourself builds trust and confidence in you so you're less affected by external conditions.

"No" is one of your most powerful boundaries. Say "no" to things that don't serve you, take you away from being your best or working toward your goals, or drain your energy and emotions. Whether you're saying "no" to others or saying "no" to yourself, you're saying "yes" to your goals, to your best self, to your truth!

Another important aspect of holding to boundaries are consequences. If you're clear with someone else and they don't honor your boundary, there must be consequences in place for them to learn that your boundary is real. With another person, that may be as simple as giving responsibility back to them for the situation they created, no longer rescuing, enabling, or bailing them out. When you don't hold to a boundary with yourself, the consequence is learning the lesson and making the necessary changes. A great method for understanding why you're not holding to a boundary with yourself is the Empowered Overthinker Method discussed in Chapter 9.

Boundaries are an important mechanism for genuine confidence and lasting success in ALL areas of your life and business.

EMPOWERED ACTION

RESOURCE

Download and complete The Power of "No" Worksheet.

EXERCISE

Get clear on your boundaries with others and have consequences for those who do not respect them.

- What is the boundary?
- What will the consequences be if that boundary is crossed?

JOURNAL

- What fears or blocks have been preventing you from holding to boundaries with yourself and others?

- What boundaries have you been allowing yourself and others to cross?

CONNECT

Share your biggest discoveries and insights in the Facebook group from what you learned in this chapter, the exercise, and journaling.

NOTES

_____

_____

_____

_____

_____

_____

_____

_____

_____

_____

_____

_____

_____

_____

CHAPTER 7: BE OPEN TO RECEIVE

PERSONAL

Growing up, I moved around A LOT! Making fast friends with people was easy, but no matter where I went or who I was friends with, I never felt like I quite fit in. There was always this underlying disconnect from others. I worked hard for people to like me, and they did, but I never felt a deeper connection with anyone. At the time, I didn't understand that the issue was with me.

I was blocking the connection because of the walls I created to protect myself from being hurt or rejected. The biggest wall was not allowing my authentic self to be exposed, only curating a version of me that I thought they'd like and not reject. Those walls kept the bad out, but also prevented the good from getting in and me from getting out. The walls I had built kept me disconnected from others. Those walls blocked me from allowing in the abundance of love, joy, and support I always wanted. One of the biggest walls that block the abundance is expectation.

This played out decades later in my marriage. For years I struggled to feel really loved and supported by my husband. I couldn't understand the problem. Of course, I thought he was the problem by not being loving or supportive. We talked, went to marriage counseling, set up talk night and date night. We even scheduled sex for a while in hopes of building our connection. Ultimately, I think those were Band-Aid fixes, never really addressing the underlying issues that each of us brought to the relationship.

It wasn't until I began my transformation journey that I understood my role in our issues, and it centered on my expectations. My expectations of how I wanted to be loved and supported by my husband didn't allow him the freedom to show up, support, and give love the way HE wanted and needed. In my mind, I was so locked into the expectation of HOW and WHO I expected him to be that I was blocking the love and support he was actually giving. I wasn't able to see, feel, or receive what he was giving because it didn't fit into my expectations.

BUSINESS

When I first met Jennifer, she was struggling both personally and professionally because of her terrible inner critic and limiting beliefs learned from the scarcity mindset of her family. When she set a goal, her critic would immediately kick in and tell her she couldn't do it because she wasn't good enough, talented, or skilled enough. Her anxiety about wanting something more would flare up for days. She was completely closed off to anything better, despite feeling like she was capable of so much more. Whatever it was that she dreamed of, she'd put resistance in her path and not allow herself to be open to receiving her goals. She never felt good enough, worthy, or deserving of what she wanted, and her critic reminded her to the point of shutdown.

Not long after working together, she finally began to love herself, something she'd never done before. Over time, her confidence and connection to herself grew, and she started believing she was good enough to make her dreams a reality. It began with allowing little things she wanted to manifest and quickly moved into allowing her big dreams to become real. The biggest goals she had resistance around were with her business as a mortgage lender, wanting a 10-unit month and $2 million closing month. Neither had happened before. Every month she set those goals, she'd sabotage herself and not allow it to happen. But once the gates of allowing herself to receive were opened, her business and life took off dramatically.

An abundance mindset became natural to her. She was open to receiving and allowing things to flow to her freely. She shifted to feeling fullness and abundance rather than lack and fear. In less than two months, she manifested her dream home which she thought she'd never have as a single mom, because of her intense worry about where the money would come from, but it was her parents' old money story blocking her from her goals. She realized she didn't have to feel or believe that way. In less than three months, she exceeded her $2 million month and had an 11-unit month! Now, she consistently hits her goal or gets close. The biggest shift for her in the allowing process was no longer taking everything personally, which used to send her down an emotional rollercoaster for days or weeks, focusing on things that fueled her inner critic and limiting beliefs. Jennifer's greatest insight is that she has finally given herself permission to be successful.

SYMPTOMS

We are the biggest blockers to our own success. We may do all the work to reach our goals, but we won't allow ourselves to get them because we aren't open to receiving abundance and success. We resist and make things harder than they need to be. In fact, you're probably a professional at over-complicating things like I did. Overcomplicating our path to success is just another form of sabotage because we believe that success is supposed to be hard.

SCARCITY

One of the most common symptoms of not being open to receive is feeling scarcity and lack permeating throughout your life and business. You feel like there's never enough time or money. There's a scarcity of other resources as well, like love, support, joy, or health. You may find fears coming up like you're not skilled, certified, trained, or experienced enough in your business to charge more, or you struggle to put yourself out there in your business at all.

Anywhere you're feeling there is a lack or not enough of something, you're in a scarcity mindset or a fear-based mindset. Underneath all of this scarcity is your root scarcity, your belief that I AM NOT ENOUGH. Whether you realize it or not, that belief is showing up everywhere in your life and business, affecting your life, business, mindset, joy, and relationships. Scarcity strangles the joy out of everything!

The belief that I AM NOT ENOUGH leads to a fear of success. If your inner critic is as bad as mine was, you're always failing to meet your own expectations, and nothing is ever good enough. So, you're a PRO at failing. The bigger issue is success. The fear that you'll not measure up or be good enough to reach your goals or maintain that level of success. Especially with money, fearing that you're not good enough or worthy of financial abundance will lead you to either block it altogether or not keep it when it comes in. Also, you fear that you'll have to give up something, some level of freedom, to stay successful because it will take a lot of "work." But if you keep doing what you're doing, it WILL take a lot of work: you are forcing it to happen because you're not ALLOWING your success to be easy.

RESISTANCE

The reason we feel like it will take so much work is due to the amount of resistance we are creating on our own. Things don't have to be hard, but our belief that we must suffer and work hard to achieve leads to our subconscious making everything more difficult. We burn out because of all this unnecessary efforting. The resistance simply comes from the sabotage and blocking ourselves from allowing abundance and our goals to come easily. They will if we let them. The biggest form of resistance we create for ourselves is expectation. Expectations of others, ourselves, outcomes, and just about anything else!

We create all of this struggle and resistance because we're out of alignment. Mainly because our beliefs are out of alignment from our truth. If I believe I'm not good enough, worthy or deserving of living my purpose and connecting to my truth, I'm certainly going to make it hard to do so. The resistance comes from scarcity and fear. It's a vicious cycle of staying stuck in the same patterns and beliefs that are constantly reinforcing each other.

SOURCE

We're also the biggest blockers to our own joy, love, health, fun, ease, and abundance, not allowing ourselves to fully experience them because of those limiting beliefs. We won't give ourselves permission to be any of the things we want. But the beliefs are only part of the reason you're blocking your own success and abundance. All of the symptoms we see, the resistance, sabotage, fear, and scarcity are external challenges created by the REAL struggle. There is only one real struggle, and it's within us. That's why all the previous methods you have used to create change in your life only worked for a little while or didn't work at all because you can't fix internal problems with external solutions. Basically, a new planner won't change how you manage your time if you're always viewing time with scarcity.

So, what is this internal struggle?

IMPOSTOR SYNDROME

The internal struggle is created by the disconnect between who we "think" we *should* be and the truth of who we are. Throughout our lives, we learn to deviate from what we want and follow the rules dictated by society, our parents and families, social norms, and any other ideas we get on who we *should* be. Also, the most common form of coping when we're young and experience pain from not being allowed to express our truth is to create walls. These walls are designed to protect us from being hurt, keeping the hurt out. But walls are not permeable, they don't let *anything* in or out. The walls also block the good from getting in and don't let us out either.

Do you ever struggle with connection, with yourself or others? Perhaps, not feeling like you fit in no matter where you go? Well, the walls are the problem. We are literally walled off from ourselves and others. This makes you feel inauthentic or like you're an impostor. Our surface self that is outside of the walls is one version of us, and who we are behind the walls can be very different. Our inability to connect with others on a deep level reflects our disconnect from ourselves. Because the walls block the love and connection from ourselves and others, they reinforce our feelings of isolation, loneliness, disconnect, and not being understood.

WALLS

Why are we disconnected from ourselves? One of the most important roles our walls have is protecting us from our past hurts. We block it out and compartmentalize our past. A trauma or rejection happened, so it's locked away behind our walls. Then, we pretend it's not there because we lack the tools to deal with it effectively. We spend a lifetime hiding part of ourselves, our wounds, scars, hurts, guilt, and shame. The more we put behind these walls, the bigger and stronger the walls get. Sometimes a trigger is big enough that it knocks a hole in the wall, and something leaks out. This disconnect from ourselves is one of the biggest sources of fuel for our limiting beliefs. All the stored junk feeds your doubt monster and inner critic because it's still part of you.

Your authentic self knows you're enough, worthy, and deserving. It does not fear lack or rejection. That part of you allows success to be easy because things are always working out for you when you're not getting in your own way. Overwhelm comes from asking the universe for what you want, doing the work to make it happen, and not allowing yourself to be open to receive it. You're so busy arguing for your old stories and limitations that it closes you off to what you want, which is another way you're blocking yourself.

SOLUTION

APPRECIATION

You can make one important shift to be open to receive the abundance you're working to create and attract: shift from resistance to ALLOWING! Most importantly, allow abundance into your life in all forms: joy, love, money, support, health, time, connection, and anything else you'd like. Be open to receiving when it comes into your life! Allow the abundance to come in without restriction or condition. That's where expectation is the biggest killer of joy. One of Tony Robbins' most powerful lessons is *trade expectation for appreciation*. Appreciate whatever is happening in the moment instead of looking at what's wrong or how it's not matching your expectations. Start by doing this at home with your partner or kids because they and you will notice a huge difference. It takes the pressure off them, and you will be way happier.

How many times have you gotten your goal, but you only saw how getting it didn't meet your expectations? So instead of celebrating your success, you see it as a failure. How many times has a friend or partner showed up to help you with something, but they didn't do it the way you do or expected it to be done? So instead of appreciating the help and feeling the support they gave you, you're upset with how they helped. Because of that, they don't feel appreciated and may not offer to assist you again, especially if you were critical of them.

ALLOW

How often do you block abundance coming into your life? Rather than accept a compliment with a simple "thank you," do you deflect by saying something nice back or pointing out something wrong instead? If someone offers help, do you say, "No, I've got it"? That's being a blocker! Those walls are blocking the good from getting in, but we must have safety and protection to dismantle the walls. That's why it's so important for your boundaries to be in place and respected by you.

Allow others to show up as they are without expectation. Be open to receiving the love, support, wisdom, and abundance they are willing to give you. Simply focus on being open to whatever that is. The simplest way to be open to receive abundance is by focusing on these two things: "yes" and "thank you." Say "yes" to accepting help, kindness, or generosity when offered. Say "thank you" when something nice is said about you or given to you. Seriously, it's that simple to be open to receiving. Start doing these two things, and you'll pave the way for *allowing* yourself to receive more.

PERMISSION

Give yourself permission to just BE who you are, the real you, by breaking down your walls, allowing the real you to get out and the abundance to come in. Yes, it's scary to be real and open and vulnerable. And sometimes you will feel hurt or rejection, but you'll experience far greater joy, love, connection, success, health, and money. The biggest wall you have is the curated, masked version of you presented to the world based on expectations. Stop worrying about what other people think and if they like you or will reject you. By honoring your boundaries, your energy and emotions are protected so you can dismantle the walls that keep your truth hidden from the world, allowing your success to flow.

EMPOWERED ACTION

RESOURCE

Download and use the Fear-Setting Exercise.

EXERCISE

MIRROR EXERCISE: look in the mirror, in your eyes (not just at yourself, but into yourself) and tell yourself I LOVE YOU until you mean it. You'll feel some discomfort and awkwardness, but push through until you really feel a shift and start breaking down some walls and resistance.

JOURNAL

TRADE EXPECTATION FOR APPRECIATION: appreciate what you're doing or who you're being in the moment, or appreciate someone else when you find yourself being critical of them due to expectations.

CONNECT

Share in the Facebook group what you've learned by saying "yes" and "thank you."

NOTES

_____

_____

_____

_____

_____

_____

_____

_____

_____

_____

_____

_____

_____

_____

_____

_____

_____

_____

_____

_____

_____

_____

_____

_____

_____

_____

_____

_____

_____

CHAPTER 8: RAISE YOUR STANDARDS

PERSONAL

Not long after I started my transformation journey, the veil was lifted from my eyes and I began to see amazing resources everywhere. All of a sudden, it seemed like I had all these options, but they were always there, I just wasn't ready to see any of them until then. So, I started consuming and became a personal development junkie! I was reading personal development books, traveling to workshops, attending events, watching webinars and masterclasses, and following gurus on social media—learning as much as I could about how to be better, do better, and have more. But I got stuck in analysis paralysis.

The problem was that I was learning a lot but not doing any of it. Learning how to improve me, my life, my mindset, but never getting around to applying the information. It was eight months after I started my cleanse, and I was stuck in a major sabotage cycle, never feeling like I knew enough or was confident enough to do what I was learning about.

Once I recognized this pattern, I looked at what I needed to do to feel good about moving forward with what I was learning. In consumption mode, I was not expecting more of myself and ended up back on autopilot with no plan or direction. I had to take a step back and evaluate what I wanted and where I wanted to go. Interestingly enough, this was also the time that I found myself seeking out new groups of people to help support my journey. No one in my circle was fast-tracking their personal development like I was, so I needed to find like-minded people. I needed a tribe of people I could connect with and learn from, but who also challenged me to be better. When I found those groups, I was able to adjust my perspective and start applying the tools and techniques I learned.

BUSINESS

For my business to succeed, I believed I needed to ride the hustle bus, working and struggling to grow. I struggled to find clients, I struggled to book sales calls, I struggled to close sales. The burnout came from doing everything that I thought I *should* be doing in my business, following all the gurus. But I didn't have the foundation, I didn't have the focus, I didn't have a plan of action, and my busyness was around pretty things, like my free journal and website.

I spent nearly a year working on my free lead magnet because I knew I needed a freebie to grow my email list. I spent 9 months of my time and energy designing a journal and paid over $2500 to get them printed. I was so focused on overdelivering an amazing product to prove my deservability, it never dawned on me that a free lead magnet needed to be simple to meet the purpose, which was *to grow my list*. Of course, the whole time I was working on the journal, I had no lead magnet, so my list and audience barely grew.

I believed that my hustle and hard work was proof of my deservability. But hard work doesn't equal success if you're focused on the wrong things. Busyness doesn't equal value or success. It just leads to exhaustion and burnout. I was riding autopilot in my business, just playing out all my old stories about money and worthiness until I decided to finally raise my standards and ask for help. I finally invested in myself and my business by working with a business coach. I'd already been burned on a high volume, low support, high investment program a few years before, so deciding to go all-in with the multiple 5-figure investment was tough to swallow, but it was time. However, as a coach, it was time to practice what I preach.

Without a doubt, it was the best investment I'd ever made to that point. Even though I was doing a lot of the what's in this book already, I was way too far down in my own stuff to have a full perspective of my life and business and who I was being in the process. I was too busy being triggered by my old junk and staying stuck in sabotage cycles. I was overcomplicating everything and dabbling in other people's ideas of business strategy rather than tapping into what felt good for me. What was missing for me was the same problem most coaches and consultants go through: helping their clients solve the problems they get stuck in themselves.

I still wasn't fully embracing my whole self and story so I could embody my authentic brand and business. My business was being built on *shoulds* rather than what was best for ME. Sound familiar? I had lots of great pieces to my business, but all those parts were disconnected instead of working together as a whole. My business reflected the disconnect that still existed in me. I needed a mentor, an outside perspective to help me focus and simplify to move forward with confidence.

SYMPTOMS

Who and what we have in our lives is reflective of where we were, not where we're going. If you want something different you have to change your expectations and standards of everything.

OLD STORIES

You're stuck because your old stories are getting more airtime in your head and in your actions than where you're going. In fact, you're addicted to your old stories, justifying and validating your thoughts, feelings, and actions by continuing to play them out. *The stories of scarcity, fear, and limitation.* Those old stories fuel the choices you make in your business and determine who you surround yourself with, the habits you engage in, and the actions you take. They make you continue to blame your parents for fucking you up emotionally and not giving you an effective toolkit, as well as not teaching you how to be confident and love yourself or take responsibility for changing things moving forward.

Those old stories make you lower your standards to feel safe and unchallenged, believe that life and success must be hard, and latch onto suffering as the price you pay for getting your goals. You believe everything must be hard so you *make* everything hard by overcomplicating things. You can't have ease, flow, or fun! You must be serious and work hard to prove your worth and value. If it's not hard, you doubt that it's real.

What are you tolerating that you know doesn't serve or support your goals? What do you accept because that's just the way it's always been?

Are you keeping an outdated toolkit that's not serving you? Engaging in habits that are keeping you stuck. Does your current tribe of people challenge and support you to be better? Or are you always the smartest, most driven, excited person in your circle of people? Are you constantly being triggered by those people because they're not supportive of where you want to go? All of those old habits, stories, and expectations are keeping you trapped in sabotage and beneath the burden of limitation.

SOURCE

EXPECTATIONS

"Standards" is a nice way of saying "expectations." Up to this point, I've been describing expectations as a negative thing that gets us into trouble, which is true. Here is where we reframe what expectations are and the role they play in your ability to create the life and business of your dreams. According to Abraham Hicks, expectations are the combination of desire and belief. You've been struggling because your desire and belief have been incongruent, which is why you keep getting more of what you don't want but believe you deserve.

You've been taught to put up with what is, so we accept things as they are, who we've been, who and what surrounds us, not to want better, do better, be better, have better. Everything in your present space reflects your standards. What you're willing to accept of yourself, of others, of your dreams and desires. That's why I mentioned in the introduction that you're great at manifesting. You're manifesting your current standards because, in spite of wanting more, they reflect where you were, not where you're going. Your standards and expectations aren't in alignment with your goals. You're manifesting what you expect, which is far below what you need to make your dreams a reality. Your expectations have been focusing on things outside your control. It's time to shift them to you in a constructive way, rather than destructive.

FOCUS

When you're feeling resistance, suffering, or struggle, you're engaging in something that is outside of what you need to be your best. Sometimes we create that resistance ourselves because we're taught that life is supposed to be hard. If it's not hard, we're doing something wrong. Basically, we tolerate continuing to play out the old stories we've been taught rather than fully grabbing onto the vision of what we want to create and who we want to be. Too busy focusing on *what is* instead of where we're going. This is the missing piece for so many and why they get stuck in preparation and planning, but rarely follow through with action. Which means, rarely getting their goals.

We learn to tune into everything outside of us rather than to our inner being, our connection to Source/God that's guiding us. You've been listening to the fear and scarcity of your ego, instead of connecting to your truth that is aligned with Source/God. Being in alignment with your truth is your connection to ease, flow, fun, love, and abundance. That's why you're still accepting less than you deserve and believing your old programming and stories. In fact, you're still arguing for and justifying your limitations and standards, rather than changing your expectations.

This looks like analysis paralysis, freebie chasing, and being a program junkie. You're learning and absorbing but not applying the tools, strategies, and techniques. Quite often, a lot of what you're learning is still *shoulds* for you because of the underlying issues we've covered in the previous chapters. These actions may not be aligned with your truth, that's why you're not following through. Some program junkies also like having a coach or a mentor to rescue them by giving them the solutions but still don't apply what they're learning as that's not their real purpose of working with someone.

SOLUTION

ELEVATE YOUR ENERGY

There's an energy to success based on who you're being. An energetic vibration that you must reach to match the energy of your goals. Basically, the more you do to support, love and express your authentic self, the easier it is to get your goals.

The biggest shift you can make for your success is to raise your energetic vibration, your energetic point of attraction. You engage in thoughts, feelings, and actions that either raise or lower your vibration. When you're out of alignment, you lower your vibration and feel resistance. When you're in alignment, feeling ease and flow, you're in a higher vibration. You must raise your vibration to match your goals. The challenge is raising your vibrational frequency and maintaining it. You do that by raising, elevating, shifting, and upgrading in all areas of your life. The fastest way to raise your vibration is by being present, incorporating more gratitude, love, joy, and fun.

Perhaps the MOST important thing you can do to ensure your success is raising your standards by upgrading and elevating you, your energy, tribe, awareness, and toolkit. This is about shifting how you're showing up and who you're being based on where you're going instead of where you are right now. Focusing on what's right in front of you keeps you stuck because what's happening now is the result of who you were being in the past.

RAISE YOUR STANDARDS

Change your relationship with expectation to be a positive thing and expecting more of yourself, your circle, your life, your business. Be open to investing in YOU! Anything worth doing requires an investment of time, money, energy, or emotion. Especially, elevate your standards for quality food and movement to nourish your body and prioritize your needs and self-care. Embrace your power of choice and choose who you are going to be in the moment: what you do, say, think, feel, and believe about yourself and the world around you.

SHIFT YOUR FOCUS

Shift your focus and allow a broad perspective of what you want in the future, not what is now. Shift your awareness to who you're being in your life and whether that is reflecting what you want to create.

CREATE ORDER

Your physical environment reflects your internal environment. But, your physical environment can have a huge impact on how you feel and who you're being. Taking control of your space by creating order and organizing helps you feel more in control of you. Plus, you're not wasting energy searching for things through the chaos. Chaos around you creates stress and distraction which lowers your energy and vibration. Even something small, like making your bed or organizing your desk can have a huge impact on your overall wellbeing.

UPGRADE YOUR TOOLKIT

You don't have to overcomplicate everything, there are easier, simpler methods to get what you want and be better. Learn new tools and skills to make that happen. Allow your life and success to be easy. Use these tools to break through the fear and doubt so you can show up consistently, which will allow you to reach your goals and grow your business. When you build the foundation to take control of you, you can become your best self and manifest your dreams. Read books, find a mentor, take courses and programs, but make sure to apply what you learn.

ELEVATE YOUR TRIBE

Surround yourself with those who challenge you to be better, not bring you down. Mind your energy and emotion, removing toxic and negative people from your circle. Are you the smartest or most driven person in your circle of people? Are you the most positive? Jim Rohn said you're the average of the five people you spend the most time with. Now, I disagree that YOU are the average, but I guarantee your results reflect the average of who you're spending the most time with.

ASK FOR HELP

You don't know everything and aren't meant to do it all alone. Be willing to ask for help and delegate because you can't do everything yourself. The fastest way to speed up your learning curve and see results is to ask for help, especially when upgrading your toolkit by learning from the mistakes and successes of others. There's no need to always reinvent the wheel.

You have the personal responsibility to align yourself with the vision of what you want to create in your life, raising your energy and vibration to match your goals. This means changing your internal management systems and your environment.

EMPOWERED ACTION

RESOURCE

Download and utilize the Control Worksheet.

EXERCISE

Evaluate your tribe: are they reflective of where you were or where you're going?

JOURNAL

What old stories are you continuing to play out? Scarcity, doubt, suffering, struggle, etc?

CONNECT

Share in the Facebook Group:

- What areas have you elevated and upgraded?
- Where have you been able to ask for help?

NOTES

_____

_____

_____

_____

_____

_____

_____

_____

_____

_____

_____

_____

_____

_____

_____

_____

_____

CHAPTER 9: TAKE YOUR POWER BACK

PERSONAL

First of all, even though I've come really far on my journey to living my best life and being successful, sabotage still happens. I still get triggered and am not always my best, but the key is to catch it quickly.

The part of my life that is still the most triggering is my marriage. Jeff hasn't been as focused on personal development as I have, so he's a bit earlier in his journey and can still have longer cycles of sabotage. This relationship is the most triggering because he's such a mirror for me, and we have similar sabotage styles. That was a huge part of our relationship, coping in unhealthy ways together as misery loves company. So, when I get frustrated with him, it's really my frustration with myself being so heavily affected by what he's doing. Yes, he's a condition that I allow to affect me, although it's decreasing every day.

Sometimes, I just feel resistance and disconnect between us. A lot of it comes from seeing him engaging in his old habits and unhealthy patterns. It triggers my expectations of him being better because I know he's capable of so much more. But those are his cycles and habits, and they are definitely not within my control.

The resistance and disconnect are coming from me focusing on what's in front of me: what is, rather than where we're going. I'm only seeing what's wrong with him or not working with us. Just like the inner critic, I've become critical of who *he* is in the present. However, when I hold space in my energy for the highest version of him, his authentic self, everything changes. There's ease and flow in our relationship because that's allowing him the freedom to show up differently and be better.

It seems simple, to just feel my connection to his highest self and view him from that perspective, but it's SO powerful. The key is getting past the stuck point of expectations or only seeing what's wrong. Anytime I'm feeling stuck in my marriage, I use the Empowered Overthinker Method to understand my trigger, learn the lesson, and get my focus back to all things amazing in my relationship with Jeff.

BUSINESS

When stepping into the realm of digital marketing, you have to build up some calluses. For some reason, once you are viewed as a business or marketer, you're no longer looked at as a person by some people. I'm sure you've seen it in the comments on sponsored ads on social media, some people can be downright mean. They don't know you or what you're about, but whatever you're doing triggers them to lash out. Honestly, those people have nothing better to do than project their negativity toward those who are doing what they are not. But, no matter how much I logically understand that what they do, think, and feel has NOTHING to do with me and everything to with them, I can still get triggered by it.

Recently, I had a very nasty Facebook message sent to me from someone who joined a challenge I ran a few weeks prior. To justify her negativity and attitude, she dramatically exaggerated the number of messages my messenger bot was sending her. As I said, I knew it had nothing to do with me personally, it's her issues. But I was still triggered! This triggered my fears of rejection and people not liking me. The anxiety created tightness in my chest, and the emotional rollercoaster started.

I cussed her up and down while I wrote a response explaining what I really thought of her shittiness, and then I deleted it. Instead, I sent a very nice and professional response, although being sure to advise her on how to unsubscribe from a bot just like an email list. Basically, I kindly shared with her how SHE has power over her own experience. But of course, as you already know, not everyone is ready to take responsibility for their own lives or hear the truth. It didn't matter. I blocked her after that. In spite of this incident triggering some of my oldest, deepest wounds, I was able to feel better in less than 30 minutes. In fact, I was completely freed of the triggered emotions by implementing my Empowered Overthinker Method.

SYMPTOMS

SABOTAGE CYCLES

You see the symptoms we've discussed so far—sabotaging yourself with perfection and procrastination or buying into distraction or excuses. Expectations fueling your disconnect and inner critic. Constantly giving your power away to external conditions and people-pleasing. You're just plain stuck. But once you become aware you're sabotaging or stuck.... then what?

What you're likely experiencing at this point is an awareness of being stuck in your sabotage cycles or knowing when you're triggered, but you don't know what to do to get out of it quickly. If you don't know what to do after you become aware of what you're doing, your critic becomes even worse. The self-judgment cycle now goes to judging the fact that you're sabotaging yourself. Thinking things like...

Why am I still sabotaging myself?

I *should* know better.

I've done all this work to change, why am I doing this again?

And so on, and so on.

Remember the reaction versus action cycles I shared in chapter 5. Your sabotage cycles are like the reaction cycle, just a bit slower in seeing the results of being triggered. Since this is a cycle of being triggered and then becoming self-critical because you're triggered, you need a pattern interrupt to break the cycle quickly and give you a constructive follow up after becoming aware that you're stuck. You need a method of quickly getting back on track and into action rather than staying stuck in sabotage, judgment, and being critical of what you're feeling and who you're being.

SOURCE

Ultimately, being triggered, experiencing negative thoughts and feelings, or being in a sabotage cycle isn't a bad thing. All of those are simply messengers that something needs to be addressed or is out of alignment with your truth. It's important to have a method for quickly getting yourself back on track, a process that works, no matter the situation or trigger.

UNBALANCED ENERGY

This isn't about forcing yourself into action because you think it's what you *should* be doing. Action is wonderful for getting your goals, but it's not the only state of being to consider when getting unstuck and moving forward. To move forward in authenticity instead of *shoulds*, we must balance our energy before taking inspired action. Everyone has both masculine and feminine energy (which has nothing to do with biological sex or gender). Action or *doing* occurs when we are utilizing our masculine energy. Feminine energy is about *being*.

Most of the time, we are thinking and doing with energy that isn't balanced, either fully masculine or fully feminine. When only using masculine energy, you're all action and can be very logical and calculated, which is great for strategy and planning. However, this can also be acting for the wrong reasons, like the expectations of others or out of fear. Choosing an action based on the wrong reasons, something that is not aligned with your truth, you may feel resistance or outright sabotage because your authentic self is saying "no." When fully in feminine energy, you get stuck in being in the present moment, which looks like acting out of your inner rebel or total shutdown from the overwhelm of being out of alignment.

SOLUTION

THE EMPOWERED OVERTHINKER METHOD

By consistently implementing the foundational five R's of the Aligned Abundance Process, you build a solid base for managing yourself and your mindset. However, it's important to have a method for identifying your trigger and reaction cycles, and consistently breaking out of them as quickly as possible. Implementing a pattern interrupt for breaking the cycles of overthinking, self-doubt, procrastination, judgment, or any negative thought cycles. I developed the Empowered Overthinker Method for working through your sabotage cycles quickly and getting into aligned action.

The Empowered Overthinker Method flows in a cycle with four distinct parts: Awareness, Ownership, Alignment, and Action.

How many times have you become aware that you're sabotaging, or that avoidance has flared up, but then you don't know what to do next? So, you start judging and beating yourself up for sabotaging and avoiding . . . here comes the inner critic. Even though you realize you're stuck or sabotaging yourself, it's easy to stay there when we don't know what to do next. I can't tell you how many times I realized I was stuck or avoiding something, then my inner critic would start judging me for it, so I felt even worse and sabotaged even more.

When working through the method, be as clear and specific as possible on your stuck point, as well as when working through each step.

The Empowered Overthinker Method

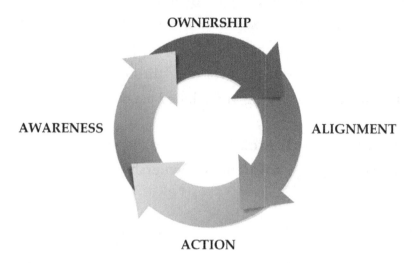

OWNERSHIP

AWARENESS

ALIGNMENT

ACTION

AWARENESS

Awareness is the greatest agent for change. Eckhart Tolle

This is about paying attention to you and being present with yourself, noticing what you're doing (or not doing) and who you're being. We are too often going through life on autopilot, just reacting and responding to the stimuli in front of us or the emotional baggage we aren't releasing. Self-awareness is a key component for learning and growth. Basically, we can't become better if we don't know what's not working.

It's time to get honest with yourself. Are you stuck or in a sabotage cycle? How are you feeling or what emotions are coming up for you? Are you triggered or sabotaging yourself?

Questions to ask yourself to gain greater awareness are:

- Where am I stuck?
- How am I stuck?
- What am I feeling?
- Who am I being?

OWNERSHIP

This is about taking responsibility for all of what you just became aware of, but with *curiosity* instead of *judgment*. How often do you blame someone or something else for being stuck? How often do you allow excuses to keep you from your goals? These are just a few of the ways we avoid taking responsibility for getting stuck and staying stuck. Also, what are you making yours that really ISN'T your responsibility? This is all the stuff you're trying to control that's not really within your control.

Either way, you're giving your power away. This is about understanding WHY you're stuck. We give away power when we don't take responsibility for what IS within our control and by taking responsibility for what's not ours. This step is all about taking back your power by getting honest and taking responsibility for your role in being stuck, while also letting go of all the stuff you've been focused on that isn't within your control.

An extremely powerful shift is to map out what you've been putting energy, attention, and emotion into using the control worksheet. The key is not to go down the judgment rabbit hole. Taking ownership is about empowerment, taking your power back, and owning where you are to move forward with clarity.

Questions to ask yourself to understand your ownership are:

- What have I been focusing on?
- How am I avoiding responsibility?
- What have I been owning that's not mine?
- What can I let go of?

ALIGNMENT

If you're stuck, you're out of alignment. The action you believe you need to do isn't in alignment with the truth of who you are, or if the action *is* in alignment, you're out of alignment elsewhere in the cycle. The biggest reason we get stuck is that we're making our decisions and acting based on *shoulds*. We are influenced by internal and external expectations of who, what, and how we *should* be. We act like the person we think we *should* be for people to like, approve, or accept us. We build our businesses based on what we see others doing in theirs and think that's what we *should* do too, and then we wonder why our business is stuck. We compare ourselves to others and feel unworthy.

Doubt comes from *shoulds* because you're not confident in your choice or action. You're not in alignment with your truth. It doesn't feel right, so you question and lack confidence.

Basically, when you're working only from your head, and not including your heart or your intuition, you're not in alignment. Headspace is good for a lot of things, but overthinkers stay there because we lack a real connection with ourselves. That's why we struggle with confidence.

In fact, this is why high-achievers and perfectionists often have the worst self-doubt. We achieve because we never feel good enough. We never feel good enough because we always do everything based on *shoulds*.

The first step to getting into alignment is to get out of your head. In your head are all the *shoulds*, limits, past junk and future fears or worries. Quickly stepping into both the present and the positive are necessary. The fastest way to do that is to *feel* gratitude or appreciation about anything. Really FEEL IT! Also, another great technique is to stop making things about you. Remember your *why* for getting your goals, the whys that are bigger than just you. Who else benefits by you showing up and getting your goals? Your family? Your clients? Maybe people you haven't even met yet will benefit from you living your purpose.

When you're feeling present and positive, this prepares you to connect to your truth. This may take a few minutes of really sitting with yourself if you've been stressed, worried, or overwhelmed. From this aligned space, ask yourself, "What do I need?" The first thought that comes up is your answer.

That's it. Based on what you need, you'll know what step you need to take to move forward.

Keep in mind that you may be surprised by the answer. Your truth may be telling you to do something totally different from what you thought was the action to take. It may seem odd or uncomfortable or send you in a direction that triggers some of your other scarcity or fear. That's okay. When the answers you get in this step are difficult to understand or feel triggering, this is an opportunity to use some of the other resources I've shared with you to help break it down into the right action for you. Use the fear-setting worksheet or release technique to work through the emotions. Journal or brain dump how to break down the answer into steps that are easier to manage.

Alignment is about checking in with YOU by connecting to your truth, which allows you to act from a place of alignment and authenticity.

Questions to ask yourself to get into alignment are:

- What am I grateful for?
- Why must I get my goals?
- What must I align to move forward?

Questions to ask yourself when you're in alignment are:

- What do I need?

ACTION

We must take action to turn our dreams into our reality. The symptom we most often notice is not taking action toward our goals: sabotage, avoidance, excuses, anything that leaves us stuck. Even if the action is aligned with our truth and the goal is something we're deeply passionate about manifesting, we may be struggling elsewhere in the cycle, not taking action because of an awareness, ownership, or alignment issue.

Taking action when we're out of alignment triggers sabotage, resistance, doubt, and the inner critic. Once you're connected to your truth and know what you need, you'll know how to move forward. This is about taking empowered action based on what you know within your soul is right. You feel confident in your decision or action because it's authentic. That's how you take inspired action instead of expected action.

When you connect to your truth, you may be surprised by what action you're telling yourself to take. The action could be to take a break, stop working on that goal, completely change focus, or even ask for help. Like all the other steps in this cycle, don't judge, overthink, or overcomplicate the step. For example, if your heart and soul are telling you in the aligned space you need rest, your action may be to take a nap or a break or disconnect from work or life for a little while. As I mentioned in the Alignment step, use the tools and resources I share in this book to dig into understanding your aligned action if it challenges you.

When you've completed the cycle, it's important to understand what you've learned to speed up the process the next time you find yourself stuck.

Questions to ask yourself to discover your aligned action are:

- What action will meet my needs?
- Is this action aligned with my truth?
- What have I learned?

Where are you stuck?

We most often notice the symptom of inaction, like avoidance, excuses, or sabotage. People tend to start the Empowered Overthinker Method with awareness. However, you can get stuck in any part of the cycle. For example, you may be avoiding a specific action because the action you've planned is not aligned with your truth. The action may be based on a *should*, and the core of your being is resisting this action because it doesn't feel right doing it or it even feels like working toward a goal that isn't really yours. Perhaps you're stuck in ownership because you haven't been taking responsibility for your thoughts, feelings, or actions. Or you're stuck because you're trying to control things or take responsibility for things that really aren't within your control. You may even be unaware of some of the underlying thoughts or emotions that are being triggered when working toward your goal.

EMPOWERED ACTION

RESOURCE

Download the Empowered Overthinker Method Worksheet and watch the video training.

EXERCISE

- Write out what you uncover around each step in the process.

    o Awareness > Ownership > Alignment > Action

- Be mindful not to question what you discover and overthink or overcomplicate the steps.

JOURNAL

What did you learn about your sabotage and stuck point by going through the method?

CONNECT

Share your most powerful lessons and insights in the Facebook Group.

NOTES

_____

_____

_____

_____

_____

_____

_____

_____

_____

_____

_____

_____

_____

_____

_____

CHAPTER 10: REDEFINING SUCCESS

PERSONAL

As a high-achiever, my whole life has been measured. My worthiness determined by a number. The number on the scale, the size on my clothes, the number in my bank account, my age, my GPA in school, standardized test scores, graduating from college as valedictorian, how many pushups I could do, how fast I ran 2 miles, how much I earn in a year, how many awards I've received, even the cost of things like cars, houses, and accessories. Everything is counted and categorized. And those measurements drove my achievement, how I defined success. Success is results-based for high-achievers, fueled by the fear of not being good enough or measuring up to the "standard."

When I finally decided to focus on me, my goal was to get healthy. I was tired of taking medications to counteract the side effects of other medications. This was the first time I wasn't losing weight to be a certain size or weight, I just wanted to feel better and reduce the number of medications I was taking. And I did just that: I focused on taking control of me, physically, emotionally, and spiritually (not all at once).

But by no longer focusing on a number, my body was free to let go of what it wanted to release. Instead of only losing 60 lbs. (which had been my goal in the past), my body released 100 lbs. Instead of stopping at a size 12 or even getting back to my college size 10, my body stabilized where it felt good between a size 6 and 8. Had I focused on a number, it would have been miserable and not in alignment with my true self. And it would have been SO hard to do!

Every diet or plan I'd "tried" in the past was only addressing the symptoms of weight and health issues, not the root emotional baggage and limiting beliefs. My transformation came from shifting my definition of success to how I felt and WHO I WAS BEING in my own life. My goal was feeling good, loving myself, having better health, and being happy. That was my new definition of success, being the best me I could be in that moment.

People ask me all the time how I lost 100 lbs. My response rattles them because it's so unexpected. They assume I'll say I followed a specific plan or worked out so many times per week. But that's not at all what I did. I tell them, "I changed WHO I WAS BEING in my life." When I did that, it was safe for my body to release the weight. The weight and health issues were just the physical manifestation of the emotional burden I was carrying. I carried that burden because I was out of alignment with my true self, living a life of *shoulds*.

BUSINESS

Every month, I set a goal and use my daily action step tracker. For years, my monthly goal was a number. Something to measure and track like the amount of income, a specific number of clients, events, or sales calls. I'd be excited at the beginning of the month, thinking YES, I can do this! I'd create my action plan and what I would do each day to make it happen and get my goal. By midmonth, if I didn't see any momentum yet, I'd start doubting myself and dig in further. Of course, I just need to work harder or do more to MAKE it happen. By month's end, my inner critic and sabotage cycles created an even bigger shit show of complete scarcity and fear-fueled panic. I was waking at 3 am panicked about bills I needed to pay or wondering where I'd find my next client. This cycle of self-triggering repeated simply because of how I set myself up to fail by consistently focusing on the wrong things for me.

When I shifted my focus to who I was being in the process rather than the outcome, I allowed myself to easily reach my goals. That's how I hit my first multiple 5-figure month, by totally forgetting the number I set for myself and just doing the actions that felt best at the time. My specific financial goal had been overlooked all month, so when I noticed it the last week of the month, I ran my numbers and was surprised because I exceeded my goal! The craziest thing is that it was easy because I allowed it to be. When I focus on the number, I immediately throw up resistance to it. When I focus on the process (how I'm showing up and who I'm being), I allow success to flow with ease and fun!

SYMPTOMS

Basically, ALL the symptoms I've addressed throughout this entire book apply to your relationship with success. But I'll wrap it up into a complete picture.

RESULTS

You've been focused on measurable results, like whether you got your expected outcome. And you rarely see your wins, only what didn't work, didn't meet your expectations, or can be improved. Despite having a long-term vision (or not), you've been focused on short-term results, especially with money. The potential for quick money may have you accepting clients who aren't ideal, business ventures promising fast money, or even still working your day job rather than taking the leap into full entrepreneurship.

Doing this may let you reach short-term goals, but it's not sustainable as you're not building a solid foundation for consistency, and you *will see* the lack of consistency in your life and business. This also keeps you in toxic hustle, with your work taking priority over everything else, including your health. Hyper-focusing on task completion becomes a must because you've procrastinated, so you work long hours and push to get it done—busyness and effort, along with results, to prove your worth.

FEAR

You know a lot from all your research and education, but you're not applying that knowledge due to analysis paralysis and a crippling fear of failure. But because you're on the hustle bus all the time, efforting and working hard, you fear success as well. If you are successful, there is no way you could sustain it as you're already exhausted and running on empty.

The fear of failure keeps you trapped in cycles of perfection, procrastination, and expectation, so you're seeing very little results for all the hard work you're doing. Carrying around the guilt and shame of past failures (or what you see as failures) fuels your inner critic. So, when you are finally willing to ask for help or guidance, you listen and then have every excuse under the sun why that won't work for you or that you can't do it. The primary focus is to avoid sabotage, but when you do sabotage, it sends you down the judgment rabbit hole. Your cycles of achievement and sabotage are keeping you blocked from tapping into your true value, worthiness, and authentic gifts. You expend excessive energy on worry and fear, leaving you exhausted and overwhelmed with performance anxiety.

SOURCE

VICTIM OF SUCCESS

All your success and achievement has been driven by the wounds of your inner child, fearing rejection and craving connection. But in giving your power away to external conditions, you've amplified feeling like a victim of your past. Basically, you've been running from your past while it's in the driver's seat of your life. No more will you be a victim and allow life to happen to you and simply respond with the beliefs and habits that are keeping you stuck.

CONDITIONAL

At the root of your belief that you're not good enough to be successful is a disconnect from yourself. This connection to your true, authentic self is the foundation for feeling confident and enough. It's how you feel a sense of fullness, love, and joy regardless of what's going on around you. But somewhere during your childhood, your ability to connect to you and trust in yourself was stifled, so you learned to use the approval of others and achievement to feel better. You were taught that your value is determined by external conditions to provide your sense of enoughness. So, you bought into the story that life is hard, hard work equals value, and you're not good enough to have what you want.

This programming is generational, and your family of origin was working with the skills, beliefs, and toolkit they were taught as well. We can identify the source of what's not working for us. Yes, you can blame your parents, but you have the power and responsibility to change that programming. You must to be successful in your life and business, to live your purpose, and be the best YOU that you are designed to be.

SOLUTION

UNCONDITIONAL

It's time to create a new definition of success as a high-performer! It will no longer be dictated by external conditions, only internal thoughts and feelings. Because you're in control of your internal environment, you're becoming unconditional. You are in control of who you want to BE in your life and how you show up. You are no longer influenced by the expectations or opinions of others. No longer doing things based on *shoulds* or comparison!

High-performers do things differently! This is about being very intentional and discriminating about where your energy and attention goes, so you no longer overwork yourself, leading to exhaustion. Especially because you are your top priority, you commit to being your best every day, which includes self-care, rest, good nutrition, exercise, and sleep.

Everything is thoughtfully chosen or decided with purpose, extending the time between a situation and you giving a response. Focus on mastery of self and being in control of you. Always make time for what works by sticking to the basics and keeping it simple, as well as your self-care plan and personal routine. Your most sacred element is being authentic and living your truth! Know that you are your most powerful resource for manifesting your dreams.

ENJOY THE JOURNEY

Your successes become more about how you feel and who you are being rather than just a result, which is of greater importance and value to your progress. We've been so programmed to only celebrate the BIG stuff—graduation, certification, a big month in business, publishing an article, getting a promotion—that we overlook the little things. But that's what it's all about, enjoying the journey because there really is NO end, no finish line to life. When you get a goal, you'll have another one lined up.

The successes are the little moments each day when you're present, in a place of peace and joy, appreciating the moment. Even if it is only short-lived. Smiling at someone, walking in nature, laughing with a child, being silly, laughing at a joke in your head, feeling the sun on your skin, smelling flowers or fresh cut grass (until you sneeze, LOL), listening to the ocean, feeling the breeze in your hair. I could go on and on. The more you celebrate your successes, especially the small ones, the more success you will create and attract. Your brain needs evidence of all the good stuff you're doing.

Another success is in changing your relationship with sabotage and your inner critic. Your inner critic isn't a bitch keeping you trapped, it's an agent notifying you of your disconnect. It's no longer about avoiding sabotage but, rather, leaning into it as a messenger. Then, you can understand that you're out of alignment and not judge where you are. Observe your triggers as an opportunity to release and heal, and then work through your sabotage cycles so you can get back on track in less time than before.

THE MIRROR EFFECT

We discussed how our inner critic uses judgment and comparison to measure ourselves against others so we stay small and feel unworthy, along with how our external relationships are a mirror reflection of our relationship with ourselves. But, judgment and the mirror effect also have a powerful role in *supporting* your success. A judgment is simply an opinion, which can be positive or negative. All the positive traits or qualities you see in others are also a mirror of your truth because you could not see them if you didn't possess them yourself. Every good thing you see in others is a reflection of you! Always remember that you're seeing YOU!

Success isn't about the results or the end game, it's about who you are being on the journey and enjoying the ride. A great indicator is feeling balance in yourself, your life, and your business. No longer determined by external conditions, your success is based on how you showed up and how you felt or what you learned during the process. Pay attention to your level of joy and connection and if you served at the highest level, are loving yourself, and being present. Build your connection and confidence so you're no longer affected by external conditions. Your sense of enoughness comes from within, so you're no longer searching for validation or approval from outside sources. Fully living your truth and purpose will come from letting go of your old stories and beliefs, shifting into this new definition of success, and enjoying the journey.

Keep in mind: most high-performers were once high-achievers who have walked the path of personal development, shifting their mindset, routines, and habits to be their best. But now, they can multiply and magnify their impact and income without working more, in fact often working less because of prioritizing and focus. This is because they are working toward their greater vision instead of individual results. They also understand the value of delegating, asking for help, and learning from experts, peers, and clients. Using the Aligned Abundance Process takes you on the path from high-achiever to high-performer and helps you redefine what success is for you.

EMPOWERED ACTION

RESOURCE

Download and use the daily Success Tracker.

EXERCISE

Write down at least one big win or success from your day on the Success Tracker.

- Make it part of your daily routine.

JOURNAL

- Brain dump all your successes, past or present.

    o Celebrate and honor your successes. It's okay to feel proud of yourself for all you've accomplished.

- With all of this evidence, why is your success inevitable?

CONNECT

Share in the Facebook group what successes you're celebrating, especially those you've forgotten about or didn't really notice before today.

NOTES

_____

_____

_____

_____

_____

_____

_____

_____

_____

_____

_____

_____

_____

YOU ARE ENOUGH

EVERYTHING YOU NEED IS INSIDE YOU

Our friends invited Jeff and me to go on a skiing and snowboarding trip with them to Vermont. My husband was an avid snowboarder, but I had only done it a few times over the course of 10 years. After renting my equipment, I wanted to warm up on the bunny slopes to get comfortable on my board, but my husband and his friend coaxed me into just going to the top of the mountain with them, promising to take the easy run down.

Waiting at the bottom of the mountain for the main chair lift, I saw clouds covering the top of the mountain. Like a scene out of a movie, the clouds parted, and the sun came out, exposing the steep slopes. My eyes continued upward, attempting to find the top of the mountain, but the chair lift disappeared up the towering mountainside. The mountain was so high that I couldn't see the end of the lift or the top of the mountain. I gulped and said to my crew, "I'm going to die!" Then I giggled to mask my near panic. They both tried to boost my confidence, telling me I'll be fine.

It was the longest chair lift ride of my life, but I successfully exited the lift without falling off my snowboard. That was my last moment of excitement as we started down the mountain. My skills only kept me from falling for a few feet at a time. By halfway down the mountain, I'd fallen more times than I could count, leaving me battered, bruised, and exhausted. Having reached my limit, I collapsed on the side of the run and started crying from frustration. I ripped off my equipment and was ready to hitch a ride with ski patrol to get to the bottom. Jeff wasn't helping at all, taunting me to get up and finish the run, making his frustration evident as well.

Our friend, who was on skis, calmly came over and told me he could help. He offered to ski behind me and let me hold onto one of his ski poles, acting as my brakes while I rode my board. As we started down the mountain with this setup, I relaxed and started riding my snowboard. I realized I had skills that I didn't know I had, and boarding came easily. In fact, I had FUN the rest of the way down!

Once we reached the bottom, I was so exhilarated by the experience because I was able to successfully accomplish my original goal of making it down the mountain without dying or killing anyone else (although, I did want to kill my husband for being such a jerk to me on the way down). Everything I needed to reach my goal was already inside me, the skills and abilities were there. However, I needed to feel confident and relax in the process, which came from support and learning a new way to do it.

The powerful lesson that came from this experience was finally understanding that everything we need is already inside. Everything you need to be your best and create the life of your dreams is already within you. You have enough of all of it! The key is to trust in yourself, take control of what's there, and focus on being your best. All the things you've been looking for outside of you—love, connection, validation, and feeling like you're enough—all come from WITHIN. That's how you're able to break free of the need for external conditions to be perfect because when what you need comes from within you become unconditional and free of expectation.

ALIGNMENT

After spending a lifetime believing that we are not enough, it can feel really uncomfortable when we start believing we *are* good enough. We jump to the conclusion that, somehow, we are arrogant or egotistical, but there is a huge difference. Believing you're enough is what creates feelings of confidence and contentment. Arrogance is driven by our ego inflating ourselves to hide the fact that, deep within, we feel insecure.

Our whole lives we're taught not to shine too brightly, to only focus on others because to think of you first is selfish, and of course, that everything must be hard. When we experience ourselves or life from a place of ease, joy, and fullness, we question it as being wrong or believe something is wrong with us, so we immediately sabotage ourselves back to our programmed conditions. Everything becomes conditional: our joy, fulfillment, enoughness, and success are dictated by external conditions like the approval or acceptance of others to feel good enough. Or you need that success or achievement to prove to yourself or others you're good enough.

Remember my story in chapter 1 about not charging enough in the early days of my business. What we charge is not based on the market. It's based on how much confidence we have, our belief in our experience and abilities, and the results we deliver. I was able to increase my rates in the first two weeks and continued to do so every few months until I reached the suggested starting amount from my coaching program simply by doing it. My confidence grew from jumping in and coaching clients.

But I stayed there for about two years until I started working with a business coach. She helped me see the value of the powerful results my clients were getting, but ultimately, I stepped into the space of fully owning and loving all of me. It was about owning my story and allowing that to align my business and messaging with my authentic brand, bringing more of my true, authentic self forward in my business, no longer doing things based on *shoulds* and expectations.

Stepping into that place of alignment and confidence allowed me to connect to the value of the results my clients were getting and adjust my pricing accordingly, which is something

I would have never thought possible when I started. And I easily enrolled clients at these much higher rates because my enoughness, abundance, and beliefs fully aligned with the value of the program. By stepping into that space of clarity and ownership, I was connecting to my clients on a deeper level, helping them achieve even more powerful shifts and growth and easily getting a return on their investment many times over.

Alignment means embracing all of you and loving yourself as whole. No more compartmentalizing and editing yourself to fit into the *shoulds* and expectations of others. No longer rejecting your past, your darkness, and your truth. This is about spending more time being the real, authentic you, speaking your truth, and living your purpose. In that place of alignment, you're able to show up to serve at the highest level, being the best parent, best partner, best business owner, and best YOU!

LISTEN TO THE MESSENGER

Your inner critic, that bitch that treats you like shit, is telling you that you're out of alignment. That voice is just a messenger urging you to reconnect to yourself to step into alignment with your truth. When your inner rebel is acting out or you're sabotaging yourself, those are just signs that you're disconnected from your truth. The key is to be an observer of that voice and your sabotage for what it is—a signal to check yourself. Rather than respond to it, sabotage, or shut down, check in with yourself and who you are being from a place of curiosity. Find out what deeper need is not being met or what old junk is being triggered and needs to be released.

It's time to let go of the old stories. They have been getting way too much airtime. In fact, you've been arguing for your limitations and buying into excuses that will keep you safe and stuck. Listen to what you're saying to yourself and others. Are you using language that is based on fear or lack? This is another way we lose sight of where we're going and get too stuck in looking at what is.

You have to recognize the signs and understand what your inner child is craving. You can no longer be so afraid of rejection and abandonment that you're never your authentic self, only the version of you that you think you *should* be to be successful or get the approval of others.

We're carrying the burdens and expectations of our parents from the perspective of our wounded inner child. Understand that your parents or family of origin loved you in the capacity and consciousness that they were and are able to at any time, not the expectation of how you feel they *should* love you. That cycle keeps us blaming them, which traps us in the hurt and powerlessness of our past. When those hurts come to the surface, it's another messenger simply telling you that you have more baggage to release. They did the best they could with the toolkit they had, but you have the power to learn the lessons and break the patterns.

YOU HAVE THE POWER

You have the POWER to choose who you want to be in your life. You choose how you show up and how you respond (if at all, not everything requires a response). Everything you need to be successful is already within you because YOU ARE ENOUGH. The key is building a solid, stable foundation of love and connection with you.

Are you brave enough to be yourself and live your truth?

Unconditionally love yourself to create your fullness and enoughness, and you'll stop looking outward to the conditions to feel like you're enough. Allow yourself to be present as much as possible to maximize your joy and experience. Enjoy the journey, have fun along the way, and amazing things happen.

Give yourself permission to love yourself and connect to your truth. Give yourself permission to be present and enjoy the journey. Give yourself permission to be successful. Give yourself permission to allow it to be easy. Give yourself permission to feel joy and have fun. Give yourself permission to shine and be your best. Give yourself permission to be you! No more pretending to be who you think you *should* be.

Have faith and trust in yourself and allow success to unfold. Remember, your job is to make sure you're managing yourself and allowing the universe to do the bulk of the work in supporting you. It's not likely to be exactly what you planned, but releasing expectations makes it so much easier and more enjoyable.

Let go of control over anything outside of you, focusing your energy and attention on being whatever your best is in that moment. That's really your only job, outside of focusing your intention and vision for what you want to create with clarity.

Allow your tribe to shift to those who support you and challenge you to be better. And be willing to ask for help because you aren't supposed to do everything yourself and you don't know everything. Be open to learning and growing.

Doing things way outside your comfort zone that challenge your old beliefs and stories, triggering that junk to come up, is a great thing. It allows it to come up and out by implementing everything in this book. While writing this book, I focused on practicing the Aligned Abundance Process daily and using the Empowered Overthinker Method when I got stuck.

Allowing that level of visibility and vulnerability triggered a lot of that junk. But it was such a blessing to get it out and feel a new level of enoughness unfold. The more you live your enoughness, the more you feel good enough. Your new cycle becomes feeling and being better, not getting trapped in the day-to-day ebb and flow, as we all have off days, and life happens. Instead, be consistent in the direction of the dreams you want to manifest and be your best self.

You have the power to be the example for those around you, elevating them by being the highest version of you and allowing that to pull them up rather than you lifting them up. Be a teacher and share what you learn. Think about all the people who will be impacted and transformed when you show up as your best and live your purpose—people you likely haven't met yet, but will be forever changed by you, either directly or indirectly because you helped someone else be their best.

EMPOWERED ACTION

RESOURCE

Download and listen to the Guided Visualization.

EXERCISE

Write your NEW STORY!

- Write it from the future, 6 months or a year from now, but in first-person present tense. If your goal is to be more present, talk about how you are being more present and what you did in the past to get you to that point.

    - Include how you've been using the techniques in this book to show up and be consistent, present, and your best.

    - What are you doing? Who are you with? Where are you? Why are you being your best? Who is benefiting? How did you get your goals?

    - Engage your senses in the story: what you see, hear, feel, taste, smell, and intuit.

- Read it every day as part of your morning routine.

JOURNAL

What was your most profound discovery when writing your new story?

- Did it trigger your critic?
- Was it easier or harder than expected?

CONNECT

Share in the Facebook group what it was like to write your new story.

NOTES

_____

_____

_____

_____

_____

_____

_____

_____

_____

_____

_____

_____

_____

_____

_____

_____

_____

_____

_____

_____

_____

_____

FINAL THOUGHTS

Your past doesn't dictate your future. You have the power to choose WHO you want to be and HOW you show up. You must DO something different to get a different result.

Whatever you're struggling with will continue to get worse until the pain of staying the same far outweighs the discomfort of change. Are you going to wait until that point?

Your inner critic is just a messenger to let you know that you're disconnected from your truth.

Your sabotage is just a messenger to let you know that you're out of alignment.

Give yourself permission to enjoy life and allow it to be easy. You have the power to create anything you desire!

Allow yourself to be open to receive abundance.

You ALWAYS have a choice!

You are in control of YOU!

YOU ARE ENOUGH!

ACKNOWLEDGMENTS

Honor to Source, God, Creator, Universe, Infinite Intelligence, Divine Light—the name doesn't matter as your magnificence abounds. You're the most absolute thing in my life and my connection to you allowed this book to manifest.

Sincere appreciation to Cori Wamsley, my brilliant writing coach, editor, and supporter who helped make this book possible. You were the voice of confidence when I was on shaky ground, assuring me that this book was not only good, but profoundly powerful. And that those who read it would be better for it!

Many thanks to marketing guru and fellow author, Lindsey Anderson, for telling me I had to finish this book. You reminded me that this book was not about me and I would be doing the world a disservice by not sharing this powerful message. Thank you for giving me a huge kick in the ass.

Deep gratitude to my amazing business mentor, Joy Bufalini, for helping me fully embrace my authentic self and let that drive my business. Your guidance helped shift my business and brand to being built upon speaking my truth. You were the catalyst for allowing the Universe to guide me to writing and releasing this book.

Reverence, love, and light to my spiritual advisor, Jason Chaussee! Thank you for calling me out on my shit and guiding me to fully sitting on the throne of the Alpha Queen. You helped me stand in my pose of uncomfortability and embrace my power through the allowing process.

Profound respect and gratitude to my amazing husband, Jeffry, for going through this journey with me. You experienced every emotion and sabotage cycle I went through to get this book finished. Thank you for pulling me away from writing and work, forcing me to take breaks when you saw that I needed it. And for grounding me when I was scattered, especially with your humor. I love you so much!!!

To my mother, for giving me the gift of my life that allowed this book to be possible. You've taught me to always find a way to push through and never give up, no matter what. Thank you for supporting me in living life on my terms and creating my own path to success.

And lastly, to my amazing clients who have shown me the greatest honor by allowing me to be a part of their journey to becoming their most powerful and aligned selves. By shining brightly and allowing your success, you're impacting the lives of so many. Your courage and lessons inspire me every day!

ABOUT THE AUTHOR

I'm a speaker, writer, coach, and strategist who helps high-achieving female entrepreneurs struggling with self-doubt, scarcity, and overthinking create the confidence and consistency they need to reach their high-level goals with ease and authenticity. My passion is to help purpose-driven women create the abundance and freedom they crave from their businesses by doing the inner work necessary for success. By aligning with their truth and growing their businesses authentically, they finally allow abundance to flow in all areas of their life and business.

As an Iraq War Veteran, recovering from PTSD and major overthinking, I've distilled down what I learned into a powerful toolkit that's simple and actionable. I've helped hundreds of entrepreneurs uncover the root issues blocking their success and given them a toolkit to stop getting in their own way and break the sabotage cycle for good because they finally believe they're GOOD ENOUGH to be successful.

At my core, I'm a rebel, so spending decades pretending to be who I thought I should be was tough. My true self always managed to leak through in amazing ways, like joining the Army and riding my own motorcycle. There's something profoundly powerful in doing things your own way. That's what is most important in the lessons I share: that you can be abundant and successful by aligning yourself and your business with your authentic self. The key is falling in love with your truth!

I live in southwestern Pennsylvania with my love and riding partner, Jeffry, along with our three cats. When not being of service to others, my hubby and I are often riding our bikes all over the country, but most often toward a beach! I adore music, travel, self-help books, learning, new experiences, and being a foodie. And I absolutely love anything that makes me laugh!

Author photo by Lauren Webster

THANK YOU

Thank you for reading! The fact that you made it here says a lot about you! You're committed to becoming your best self and being an aligned, purpose-driven business owner who impacts lives! Let this be the start of our amazing relationship.

LET'S CHAT

If it's time for you to be part of the Empowered Overthinker movement and create your own Aligned Abundance, you can go to my website to learn more and get on my calendar. Hop over to https://www.stacyraske.com. I'm excited to chat with you!

JOIN THE MOVEMENT

I'm excited to hear more about your vision and business, along with the impact you want to have in the world. Find me on Facebook (https://www.facebook.com/stacy.raske), follow my journey and travels on Instagram (https://www.instagram.com/stacy.raske). And of course, join my Aligned Abundance Lab Facebook group (https://www.facebook.com/groups/alignedabundancelab).

It's time to give yourself permission to be YOU and finally believe you're GOOD ENOUGH!!!

Stacy Raske Martin